I0414541

Growing Up White in America

Growing Up White in America

✦

Experiences with Race

Bem P. Allen

iUniverse, Inc.
New York Lincoln Shanghai

Growing Up White in America
Experiences with Race

Copyright © 2007 by Bem P. Allen

All rights reserved. No part of this book may be used or reproduced by any means, graphic, electronic, or mechanical, including photocopying, recording, taping or by any information storage retrieval system without the written permission of the publisher except in the case of brief quotations embodied in critical articles and reviews.

iUniverse books may be ordered through booksellers or by contacting:

iUniverse
2021 Pine Lake Road, Suite 100
Lincoln, NE 68512
www.iuniverse.com
1-800-Authors (1-800-288-4677)

The views expressed in this work are solely those of the author and do not necessarily reflect the views of the publisher, and the publisher hereby disclaims any responsibility for them.

ISBN: 978-0-595-44492-2 (pbk)
ISBN: 978-0-595-88818-4 (ebk)

Printed in the United States of America

Contents

Acknowledgements and Dedication

Heartfelt thanks are due Paula Allen, Margaret Allen Caulkins, Kathleen Allen, and Bem Allen III for their thoughtful, insightful, and immensely helpful comments of drafts of this book.

To my students.

Preface

I've studied racial prejudice for more than 40 years. That includes a 37 and a half-year university career and the last years of my graduate school training. Although this book is not about my research—the next several sentences contain almost all I've written about it here—an incident occurred during one of my research talks that put me on the path to writing this book. In the spring of 2005, as a part of my department's weekly symposium on psychology topics, I delivered a talk on racial prejudice to a mostly student audience. The experiments I talked about involved presenting my mostly white research participants with a list of 15 words each referring to violent men, for example, murderer, assailant, and rapist. Later they studied a list of 15 American ethnic names: Mexican American, Korean American, Irish American and others, but not including African American. On a subsequent memory test, research participants were reliably more likely to report having "seen" African American on the ethnic names list, if they had previously studied the violent men list than if it had been replaced with a neutral list. Reporting an item suggested by a studied list, but not actually on the list, is called a "false memory." These results and those of many other experiments suggest that "violent men" and "black men" are linked in many people's minds.

When I finished the talk and expressed a willingness to answer questions, one of the several young, black men in the audience raised his hand. He wondered why a white man had spent most of his life contemplating, researching, and talking about racial prejudice. Although there were several answers to the question, my parents came immediately to mind. Their families were distantly related—Daddy was named after Mama's great uncle, Bem Price—and both settled in the Confederate South before the Civil War. Their position regarding race was unique and complex. I'll return to it in due course. Here it is sufficient to indicate that racial prejudice was a major part of their worldviews. Under the influence of this knowledge, I responded to the young man's question with, "When your parents are extreme on an important issue, you either embrace their position or oppose it." As I grew up I developed beliefs about race that are very different from those of my parents. This book is about the evolution of my thinking on race that began with the collision between my early experiences with the issue and my parents' unique brand of bigotry. I hope to show that growing up white in America has a pervasive influence on white folks that continues to profoundly impact black folks.

1

Small Town USA

Very few memories of my birthplace—Vincennes, Indiana—are still with me today. Our family was there for only five years, 1940 to 1945. Early emotional memories tend to stick with us longer than our first memories about events in our lives. Photographs of Mama taken during that time haven't helped me conjure what she was like back then. Still I somehow sense that she was gentler, warmer, and more attentive than she became when my two sisters and I reached elementary school age. As far as I can recall, there were no black people in the town, thus, no stimuli for the reactions that came to characterize her in my mind as I approached adulthood.

Daddy was a very quiet, almost stoic, man. Unlike Mama, he was among the first members of his extended family to receive a college education. He did very well both academically and socially at his little military college. Upon graduation he accepted a position at Phillips Petroleum as an electrical engineer. By the time my sisters and I arrived, and World War II began, we were doing better than most families in that post-Great Depression era. But recollections of my father's nature at that time are more ethereal than those of my mother. As was true for my mother, there were precious few occurrences in our small Mid-Western town that might have inspired comments about or reactions to black people.

Sometime during World War II, our Grandmother, Mama's mother, became a part of our lives. She was a stately and refined Southern Matriarch who tended to become ill at the mere thought of violence. "Polly," as we called her, would become the most important person in my life. While she shared my parents' views about race, she was, in a sense, even more extreme in her beliefs.

During 1945 we moved to Kosse, an East Texas town of about 800 people, where Daddy was born and reared. He was attempting to live out a dream of triumphantly returning to his hometown as co-owner of a successful butane/propane gas business. He and his brother hoped to persuade people in the town and the surrounding countryside that gas for heating and cooking was more economical and efficient than electricity and wood. Daddy provided the expertise and most of the money for trucks and tanks. The venture depleted the considerable savings he accumulated during his time at Phillips. Had he succeeded, his life and ours would have been quite different. Sadly it failed.

Undaunted, Daddy parlayed his knowledge of gas appliances into a sales position with Dearborn Stove Company. Very quickly he became number two in sales of gas home heaters, commanding a phenomenal salary for the time, $10,000 annually. During the late 1940s and early 1950s we became affluent by most standards. As a result, Mama was able to hire a "colored" maid to do the housework and, more importantly, to obey her commands and pay her homage. Saddi, as I shall call her, was a black woman, apparently in her thirties, whose orientation to compliance was exceeded only by her hesitance to speak. I suspected that Mama selected her on the basis of these two traits rather than her domestic skills. For the first time, my sisters and I had daily contact with a black person.

Perhaps influenced by Mama's anecdotes about Kosse, I recall that our house was a mansion, sufficiently large and grand to require servants. It had a butler's pantry that separated a very large kitchen from a sumptuous dinning room. A large library/living room and a bedroom with a bathroom constituted the rest of the downstairs. Upstairs was composed of three bedrooms and a bathroom. The house was rented and one of the bedrooms contained possessions of the owner stored behind a padlocked door. This room was scary and intriguing at the same time. I daydreamed of breaking into it and discovering treasures and maybe even dead bodies.

Kosse provided evidence that there is at least a kernel of truth to almost every stereotype, in this case the one about people in small towns knowing each other's business. Every white person knew almost all other white people, and many of the black people who regularly came to town. That was especially true of one person, the telephone operator. Mabel, as I shall call her, knew more about everyone in town than anyone else, because she manually connected callers to recipients of calls and could listen in on conversations. Of course, during the early 1940s, not everyone had a phone. I would estimate that from 40 to 60 percent of Kosse's approximately 800 inhabitants had phones. Thus, what Mabel knew about people who had no phone came from overhearing scuttlebutt about them during phone-owner conversations. Our phone itself was an interesting period piece. It was a big, rectangular, wooden box with bells centered at the top, a speaker horn in the middle, a listening horn wired to one side, and a crank that had to be turned to contact the operator. In the eyes of a young boy, it was a marvel of modern technology.

My sisters and I occupied one of the two available upstairs bedrooms and our parents the other. I have very pleasant memories of this room as it included a portal to freedoms unlike any we would experience until adulthood. One of the room's windows opened to a roof on which lay a large branch of a massive mulberry tree. Being sent to our room because of naughty behavior was like Brer Rabbit being thrown into the briar patch. As soon as Mama escorted us into the room, left and slammed the door behind her, we scurried to the window and were down the Mulberry tree in what seemed like seconds. It was the best of several sources of freedom available to us.

That Mulberry tree had other uses, one of which allowed us to experiment in the mistreatment of a person we had come to regard as a lesser being. The great gulf between Saddi and Mama, who rarely set foot out of the kitchen, must have subtly invaded into our emotions if not our consciousness. To Daddy, whose sales job kept on the road all week, Saddi seemed not to exist. Whatever the reasons, we concocted a way to "fool" Saddi. After some discussion, we decided we would test a belief conveyed by our parents that Mulberries were worm infested and evil tasting. Out of sight in the shadows of the house we carefully crushed many Mulberries and poured the juice into a Grapette bottle that we recapped. With childish anticipation we huddled close as we interrupted Saddi's kitchen chores. I can't remember who offered her the bottle, but she accepted it without hesitation and quaffed its contents as we watched with fascination. Nothing happened. She neither seemed to enjoy it nor found it disgusting. We retreated in disappointment without thinking about the implications of what we had done, much less discussing it. In retrospect, I realized that we pretended kindness when our actual intent was cruelty. We could not have acted as we did had we not sensed it was acceptable.

Partly because of the freedom and autonomy we experienced, living in Kosse was a continuing opportunity to learn, though many of the lessons were lost on us until years later. A large area surrounded our house over which we could roam and explore. On one side of the house, a fence enclosed a pasture that contained horses so tame they would sidle up to the gate and allow us to jump on their bare backs for a joy ride. Once, when I fell off one of the horses, it obediently halted and stood patiently while I yanked on its mane until I was able to remount. On another occasion, I was riding outside of the pasture and, unbeknownst to me, it was dinnertime for my steed. He suddenly lurched forward into a full gallop and headed for his stable. I was caught sitting up straight hanging onto the animal's mane for dear life. Unfortunately, that put me at the height of a metal clothesline that caught me neatly between the lips of my open mouth. I was yanked from my mount and dumped onto the hard ground in an undignified heap. Being unscathed, except for rust marks on both sides of my mouth, I came to regard the incident as high adventure.

On the other side of our house, a dirt road began at the paved highway bordering on our front yard and wound into the country through endless fields of cotton. I spent hours watching what happened on and around that road. About weekly, I could see our across-the-road neighbor wash her family's clothes in a large cauldron atop a wood fire. Amid steam and smoke, she stirred the waterlogged clothes with what looked like an ax handle. It was the only washing "machine" poor white folks could afford. But what about black folks? Almost all of them were poor. How did they handle life's everyday tasks? An answer to this question was difficult to come by, as there were few if any black people living in town. My knowledge of blacks outside the context of our house was restricted to the few occasionally traveling down the road toward town aboard mule-driven buckboards—wooden wagons with metal-rimed wooden wheels and a single seat supported by springs. They passed without looking at me or doing anything that would reveal what their lives were like. That changed one day when a friend and I watched a black man and his young son approach us bouncing about on the spring-mounted seat. Suddenly, my friend began to shout the "n" word at the little boy and his father. It seemed exciting so I joined in. The boy's father fixed his gaze ahead and did not react. However, the little boy faced us and shouted, "white trash, white trash." Perhaps because of my friend's reaction—more intense shouting of the "n" word—I sensed that we were being condemned in no uncertain terms. But the phrase was new to me. Later, when I related the incident to Mama, I asked for the meaning of the highly emotional phrase. She replied simply, "White trash is as low as you can get."

Thereafter, I avoided any action that I imagined might get me classed as "white trash." That included use of the "n" word. I never heard my parents utter the word; they taught my sisters and I to use "colored" in reference to black people. As I grew up, I came to realize that the kind of racism expressed by my parents and my grandmother was a sort of paternalistic, condescending variation of the better-known, overtly hateful and venomous sort promoted by the Ku Klux Klan. My parents' position will become clearer when I discuss our confrontations as I grew to young adulthood.

Neither exposure to black women, nor the encounter on the dirt road, was of any help in understanding how whites regarded black men. Later I was to meet a black man, I shall call James, who was known as the strongest man in the county. James had only one arm. The other was rumored to have been lost in a cotton gin accident. But what an arm it was. Local legend had it that James could pick up a bail of cotton with that massively muscular appendage. Having heard these stories about James, I was excited that he was coming to our house to help carry a piano into our living room. James picked one end of the huge instrument while two white men lifted the other end. As they proceeded up the front stairs into the house, James seemed to move effortlessly while the other two men grunted, strained and occasionally staggered. James lived up to his billing. That was the day I began to incorporate the stereotype that black men are physically strong.

But what else were they? I can't remember the source of an incident that was to plant the seeds for another belief about black men. A white friend of my family's ran a small store with some groceries and a variety of odds and ends. Supposedly, one day he was confronted with a black man who became belligerent over a disagreement about a sales transaction. The proprietor, a man I admired for his funny stories and lessons about manhood, was said to have screamed at the black man, "If I can't kill you with my bare hands, I'll get a gun!" How could a minor disagreement lead to a death threat? It was to become clear that black men, who were believed to be prone to meanness and violence, were never to regard white people with other than deference and subservience. Should a black man insult a white man, or just become "uppity," the latter was obligated to threaten deadly violence lest the black man, because of his assumed inherent viciousness, become a threat to the entire white community. Of course, if a black man looked at a white woman for longer than could be measured in milliseconds, the threat was often bypassed in favor of beatings or worse.

Beginning at the time we moved to Kosse, my elderly grandfather needed a nursemaid. A black woman named Sue Hill was hired to fill that role, though she was older than his eighty some-odd years. Sue was very distinctive in appearance, beginning with a slim body that made her seem rather frail, an illusion that evaporated when she was observed working about Grandfather's house (see the picture on the cover: my father is on the top row, far left, my grandfather next to him in the middle, and Sue just below him; the others are aunts and uncles). Even today I can easily picture the richly creased, dark skin of her face, but her hair is difficult to conjure as it was often hidden beneath a headscarf. Until she smiled and showed her joyful side, she looked very solemn and serious, a person who commanded respect. And respect was what she received from family members, along with a large measure of affection. Her presence, front and center, in the cover photo taken at a family reunion, bares witness to the esteem with which she was held. I can't imagine them being photographed with any other black person. My family, like many other white people, could point to exceptional black individuals who deserved to be well thought of, if not treated as equals. If accused of harboring prejudice, whites would name these "exceptions" and claim to have treated them well. Later, I'll consider the impact on people of color who are regarded as exceptions.

My clearest recollection of Sue comes from a return to Kosse after we had moved. It was another family reunion with all of our cousins. After the obligatory huge meal, with much excitement, my cousins began begging their parents and mine to let us visit Sue at her country cabin. Permission was granted. We all piled into cars and paraded down dirt roads enshrouded in dust. When we arrived at a run-down, bare-boarded shack, my cousins tumbled out of the cars and gathered around the front door, knocking wildly. Slowly Sue opened the door and emerged from the shadows in a faded cotton dress. Her expression at first reflected puzzlement, but quickly morphed into pure pleasure as she recognized the faces of the children now surrounding her. She exclaimed, "My chilluns is here!" as they reached out to touch her and help her down the wobbly stairs. I see myself standing in the background as my cousins each got a hug and a kiss from Sue. I felt scared. I don't think I had ever touched a black person before. Her enthusiasm in embracing my cousins made me even more hesitant to step forward. Finally, though, I got my turn. How I received her hug and kiss has escaped my memory.

That day Sue showed what a remarkable person she was. Every child with whom she had contact was one of her "chilluns." Every person she knew well was family to her. Sue's great strength was perfectly matched by her gentle and sweet nature. While she was present, her total acceptance and genuine affection for everyone dissolved the thick line that divided black and white.

Enough was known about Sue to suggest that her sterling nature was developed and maintained despite a horrendous past. She was reputed to be past 100 when she died during the early 1950s. Thus, she must have been born into slavery. The abject poverty and deprivation that characterized her life seemed only to nurture her exemplary ability to see all people as worthy of affection. Her life was a tribute to the extraordinary resilience of the human spirit.

2

Big Town USA: Jacinto City

By 1950, we had abandoned Kosse for what might be regarded as a suburb of Houston, Texas. Because of the oil industry and the ship channel—which fed the USA's number one port in terms of cargo-tonnage handled—Houston was expected to be the country's largest city by the year 2000. These high expectations brought thousands of post-war job seekers to greater Houston, including Daddy in his quest for even more success at gas-stove sales.

We settled into a cinder block house, one of the many thousands built to accommodate returning World War II soldiers and their families. It was solid and modern, but small. Our kitchen was about the size of the butler's pantry in our Kosse house. It adjoined a comfortable living-dinning room area that connected to a back porch with walls of small, rectangular glass-panes that could be cranked to opened or closed positions. There was also a single bathroom and two bedrooms. Our parents took the larger bedroom with my sisters and I crammed into the smaller one. Later space became even more precious when Polly joined us and shared our cramped quarters. When I reached age eleven, Mama thought it was improper for me to be bunking with females so I was moved to the back porch. There I froze in the winter and boiled in the summer, but it was my own space. I felt blessed.

As he did in other times during my childhood, my father showed his creativity. Using tin-can tops, he fashioned a thermostat to regulate the only fan that cooled our house. Because I loved listening to the radio, but lived in a space too small to accommodate one, he fashioned a miniature radio receiver out of crystal, wire, and plastic and connected headphones to it. I could listen to the Lone Ranger, Jack Benny, broadcasts of the

Houston Buffalo baseball team and other favorites by simply moving a stylus over the crystal until I found the desired station.

We lived next door to a strong and domineering man and his earth-mother wife. Their son became my best friend. Today, Todd, as I shall call him, would be labeled a "wannabe." He loved American Indians and, as much as he could, lived their life as depicted in the movies and children's books of the time. Because he wore as few clothes as possible, virtually year-round exposure to the sun gave him the ruddy look of an Indian. While his parents were able to get him into a shirt and pants during school hours, he took every opportunity to discard his shoes. Todd's unshod feet became so calloused that he could walk on any surface without discomfort, including the blazing-hot summer sidewalk and gravel roads composed of sharp stones. By the time he entered the fifth grade his toes were spread so wide that only over-sized shoes would fit him. It was Todd who taught me to love the woods that were near by and to explore them thoroughly.

Todd's father was a fine man. Nevertheless, like many of us even today, he relied heavily on stereotypes to construct his social reality. Every Friday night we huddled around his small black and white TV to watch wrestling, which was a local event as was every other program available in the Houston area. On these occasions, I "learned" about non-white people, particularly "Orientals." The major theme of wrestling was much the same then as it is now. There were heroes and villains, the former to be cheered and the latter excoriated by all who attended a match, including "little old ladies" purposely seated on the front row. Heroes during this time were almost all whites while "Japanese" villains were popular after World War II. In fact, any Asian-looking man passed for "Japanese" as the requirement for certain identification was simple: anyone with "slanty" eyes was a "Jap." As a case in point, during high school, my classmates included some white brothers with "slanty eyes." Someone referred to them as "Japs," an appellation they embraced in the same spirit as others "honored" with a nickname.

During those Friday evening wrestling matches, I learned that "Japs" were inscrutable: their slanty eyes concealed malevolent intentions, as did their stoic demeanor. They were, therefore, underhanded, sly, and bent on deceiving Occidentals for the purpose of gaining an advantage over them. More importantly, all of them were that way, while white people—more generally one's own group—were "good," which included forthright, trustworthy, cool-headed and benevolent. Never mind that one might know some "good Japs" (exceptions) and members of any group, white or not, readily acknowledge that there is constant strife among own-group members owing to the existence of many "black sheep" in their ranks. Although the manifestations may be relatively subtle these days, almost all of us at least occasionally fall into the "*they* are all alike" trap. Not only are "they" alike in appearance, but also in beliefs, traits, and values. It's a quick and dirty way to assess other-group members: energy expended on thinking is minimized and the simplified view of the "other" allows one to quickly dismiss them. Not until I was in college did I begin to question the validity of this and other sources of stereotypes.

I saw Todd only a few times after we left Jacinto City. We were on opposite sides of the line of scrimmage when his high school football team played mine during my senior year. I was an ordinary player; he was an all-star center. Some few years before or after this encounter, I visited him in Jacinto City. Todd was in his garage working on a new American Indian bow, one of the many he possessed. As usual, he was unshod and looked very much like an Indian. I wondered no more about whether his identification as an Indian was genuine. Perhaps he has Indian heritage, as do so many white Americans, including my wife. Or maybe identity transcends "race" or ethnicity such that if one is steeped in a culture, because one is reared in it or because one admires it in the extreme, he or she becomes a full-fledged member of the group associated with the culture. It is known that American Indians adopted white children they captured. They also accepted black escapees from slavery as full-fledged members of their tribes. These non-Indians became Indians in spirit and soul (for more information, Google or Ask "Black Seminole").

But what are the limits of wannabe-ism? An American Indian I heard speak at a recent convention related how he encountered some German tourists who were wannabe Indians. They maneuvered him into a car, took him to a remote place, and just when he began to fear for his life, to his astonishment, they commenced speaking to him in his tribal language. Before the evening was over, he found that they knew almost as much about his tribe as he did. Were they "real" Indians? One should not be too quick to say "no." It is philosophically complicated.

"Wannabe" most often refers to white people who want to be black. This group has, since at least the 1930s, included white musicians who came to understand that much of the greatest of American music has its roots in the contributions of black musicians. More recently it has come to include aspiring white athletes who so strongly believe that blacks are "the real" athletes that they begin to "act black" and white-teen rap fans that dress, speak and mimic (stereotypical) "black behavior." Quite recently I heard about an extraordinary wannabe, a white teenage girl living in an integrated upper-middle class neighborhood who declared that she wanted to be "black and poor"! She dated only black boys because "they accept over-weight girls."

The wannabe phenomenon highlights a fascinating ambivalence about blacks in the minds of whites. On the one hand, displays of explicit and overt prejudice have become increasingly rare over time. On the other hand, subtle, non-consciously expressed forms of prejudice, that are accessible only by use of sophisticated techniques, have persisted across time. Against this background, many whites will declare that racism is a thing of the past. As evidence for this assertion they may point to their admiration for a number of black public figures. True to their mixed feelings, in almost the same breath, they may make a contradictory disclosure, such as that they moved from a neighborhood that was "becoming black."

Before one concludes that ambivalence is better than out and out rejection, it is helpful to remember that Jews were the Nazis' worthy opponents. The Nazi SS included "Jewologists" ("experts" on Jews and their culture). Just as archeologists come to admire and respect members of the ancient societies they study, SS "Jewologists" were proud to proclaim that Jews were responsible for many notable contributions to art, science, and business (while at the same time, they burned books by Jewish authors, scientists, and philosophers). These successes on the part of a non-Aryan people, embedded in the German sphere of influence, constituted part of the reason they were marked for extinction. Adolf Eichmann, who was executed for planning and implementing the transportation of Jews to Nazi death camps, was a self-proclaimed "Jewologist." Does this mean that ambivalence inevitably leads to genocide? Certainly not, but the positive side of ambivalence may sustain the negative side.

3

Big Town USA: Park Place

During our time in Jacinto City, Mama had put her elementary school teaching degree to use for the first time in many years. Previously, she had been a homemaker, which was traditional for white middle-class women of her generation. While she toiled at three jobs—child-care, house-cleaner/cook and teacher—Daddy worked at Sears in the complaint department. He had lost his gas-stove sales job soon after we arrived in Jacinto City due to the diversion of steel to the Korean War effort. Even with both parents and Polly—a licensed social worker—contributing to the family income, I sensed that life was not good. Three growing children and three adults stuffed into a tiny house was at least uncomfortable, if not out-and-out stressful.

The promise of a better life led our parents to consider Houston proper. After Mama successfully found an attractive teaching position in the vicinity of East Houston, and Daddy landed a transfer to a Sears store in the same general area, they found a nice home in the Park Place section of East Houston. The house was centered behind a circular driveway on a lot that measured an acre and a sixteenth. Enclosed within the driveway was a field of grass large enough to accommodate touch football games, though the limbs of two palm trees just within the bounds of the driveway scratched and bloodied at least a few players during each game. Looking at the house from the street, the front was composed of a screened-in porch. An open porch continued to the left and was attached to a carport. Still further to the left and more to the front was a cement pond that, when filled with rain, seemed to attract snakes. Once I saw a Coral snake, America's deadliest, slither along the planks of slate that formed the border of the pond. When I told Mama, she taught me a rhyme to protect me in the future:

"red and yellow kills a fellow." Even farther to the left of the house, just beyond the pond, was a ravine full of lush growth ranging from berry bushes to poison ivy. Its presence allowed me to continue my now solitary explorations of nature.

The lot was covered with many trees, some pine, some oak, and one magnificent Magnolia tree. Most were covered with moss. Cleaning up that moss and mowing the lawn were my main chores. I was also hole-digger par excellent. Mama and Polly would spend what seemed like hours coercing me into digging holes for their flowers and other plants. I can still see the two of them standing back as I dug. They would comment in hushed tones about my outstanding hole-digging skills, acting as if I couldn't hear them. Later, during my psychology training, I marveled at how well they understood that "accidentally" overheard social influence attempts are especially effective.

Daddy did some "fixit" chores around the house and Mama did the rest. One of my sisters cannot recall any chores that she and my other sister regularly performed. Perhaps it was because Mama always believed that menial tasks were beneath aristocratic, southern ladies in whose number she counted herself, as well as her daughters. Though our fall from relative wealth caused her to stoop to housework and other drudgery, she believed that her daughters would meet a better fate.

My younger sister was enrolled in a nearby elementary school and my oldest sister in the local high school. I had to go to the area's junior high, a real "blackboard jungle," but without anyone who resembled Sidney Poitier. Black people, including children, were completely segregated, occupying mostly the Third, Fourth and Fifth Wards of Houston. However, Mexican Americans, then called Mexicans and more recently Tejanos, were fully integrated into the schools, but segregated elsewhere. This arrangement is puzzling. It became even more so when I discussed school segregation with a colleague whose family has owned land in Texas under several of its six flags, beginning with Spain's. She and other Latinos were placed in separate Corpus Christi schools, while almost all of the few blacks in town attended white schools. Perhaps it was that Latinos were greater in numbers in Corpus Christi compared to Houston, and, thus, more threatening to the white majority. Money was probably a factor also. It would have been costly to build separate schools for the relatively few Latinos in Houston, but not for the much larger number in Corpus Christi. Finally, historically, the further "south" you go in Texas the greater the bias against Latinos.

Or maybe I should say, "southwest." During the early to mid-1950s I played chaperone to my older sister and her boyfriend during a trip to visit his aunt, uncle, and cousins who lived in the extreme southwestern part of Texas, very near the Mexican border. Our hosts were affluent landowners whose sprawling ranch house included quarters for a Mexican nanny ("Mexican" is used here, rather than the more general "Latino," as almost all Spanish speaking people in and around the town had Mexican roots). The boyfriend's cousins were all fluent in Spanish as well as English, as their nanny taught them the former during the course of caring for them.

The boyfriend's uncle was the most important man in town. Local Mexicans showed him a level of respect that bordered on veneration. He was the local Patron. Though the power he wielded over the Mexican population in the town was apparent almost immediately, I was still amazed when an incident concretely illustrated his ascendancy. The boyfriend's teenage cousin showed me around town in an open jeep. As he drove his head was rotating this way and that so that he wouldn't miss waving at his many friends. At one point he was swiveled around about 90 degrees waving, shouting and honking his horn at what must have been a special friend. Before he could reorient himself in order to address what was in front of him, he collided with a brand new automobile driven by a Mexican man. No one was hurt. The man emerged from his badly mangled car before we could recover our composure. Hat in hand, he approached "Mr. Armstrong" (not the actual surname of the offending teen driver) and offered his apologies. Magnanimously, the boy indicated that he was at fault, not the man whose new car he had bashed, and that his father would take care of everything. The victim of teenage distraction acknowledged that he had no doubt the Patron would fix his car. He seemed sorry to have gotten in the way. I could only wonder what would have happened to the man had he dared to protest the destruction of his prized new car at the hands of the Patron's careless son.

Historically, discrimination against blacks has occurred throughout Texas, but has been milder where there their numbers are small. Until the 1960s, black people in Houston were as invisible as Ralph Ellison in New York City during the 1940s. In the 1950s, Houston had both *de jure* and *de facto* codes to enforce segregation of drinking fountains, housing, schools, restaurants, churches, swimming pools, parks (except in black neighborhoods), and jobs. As to the latter, except in their own communities, blacks were largely confined to manual labor. In addition, whites had almost all of the city and state jobs and political offices. There was not much difference between Houston and Oxford, Mississippi: after all, both are located in former Confederate states. In both places, blacks were excluded from involvement in most of their cities' meaningful, important, and powerful institutions and pursuits.

Some black people living in Houston during the 1950s did eventually lead acclaimed lives. Boxer George Foreman and U. S. Representative Barbara Jordan are examples. Foreman was twice world heavyweight champion and Jordan will always be remembered for her eloquent commentary on the Constitution during the Watergate hearings. One can only wonder how many talented black Houstonians died in obscurity.

Deady Junior High School is now a middle school and its students' academic performance is among the poorest in the area. Back in the early to mid 1950s when I attended the school, it seemed that gangs were the most severe problem. The "rule" that gangs attack mostly members of their own ethnic group was probably stronger during the 1950s than it is today. The white and Latino gangs didn't bother each other, probably because, if they did, someone would die. But each was a danger to its own group.

My own fear of the white gangs made me want to be anywhere but at Deady. But my feelings changed from scared to extremely vulnerable when I saw two of the most respected white boys—one big, strong and a fierce fighter—not resisting when attacked by white gang members. I found my solution in the old saw, "If you can't beat 'em join 'em." I began to act like a gangster. To be bad in that time meant carrying a switchblade knife and wearing cool shoes that made a lot of noise. The latter was accomplished by lining the soles and heels with metal taps. When I plied the halls of Deady I must have sounded like an AK-47 going off. My rationale was to look so bad no one would mess with me.

Mama noticed the change in me. Though she was very busy she sensed that something was wrong, perhaps aided by her likely knowledge of my collaboration with a neighborhood friend in blowing up a cranky woman's mailbox. Mama became more questioning of my activities. Even so she didn't know that I also was involved in vandalism (for example, throwing paint-filled eggs at other people houses). I also became insolent. On one occasion I so angered my father that he chased me … but, only for a short distance. Perhaps looking to get an emotional reaction from him, an accomplishment that I could not remember having achieved before, I said something that insulted his masculinity. I was thrilled at his reaction and disappointed that it was so short-lived.

Trying to look bad didn't work. You get accepted as a gangster by fighting. One day I got into fist fights with three other pretenders at being bad. No one was hurt, but, being unable to face daily fights, I looked for another way to get the gangsters to leave me alone. It was clear that nobody messed with the jocks. I took up football. As a result I was more regularly beaten up than I would have been had I continued the gangster pose. Nevertheless, not only did being a football player free me from the fear of the gangs, it provided the camaraderie an early teen needs to feel accepted and secure. My fellow players became my best friends and constitute most of the old friends I remain in contact with these days.

Thinking about my "gangster period" reminds me of a fact that I believe escapes most white folks: historically, in the USA, white gangsters—more generally white criminals—have been the problem. As poor whites—many from families recently immigrating to this country—moved toward affluence, they abandoned the gangs. Thus, today, it may appear that white gangs don't exist. In fact, they do. They exist in significant numbers among some Irish in the Boston area, among some Russian immigrants in New York and California, and among some of the various Eastern European groups that have recently immigrated to the USA.

But, still, it may seem that black and Latino gangs predominate today. First, there are other non-white gangs taking hold in the USA. Gangs from East and Southeast Asia have a foothold in America. Second, while Latino youth gangs date to the 1950's, their activities historically have been largely restricted to their own neighborhoods. More recently the "Mexican Mafia," a group that is unaligned with USA Latino gangs, are terrorizing blacks and others in California.

Growing up in Houston, I never heard of black gangs. I'll focus on the Houston police later, but here it is sufficient to say that if more than a couple of black teens gathered on a street corner—especially outside their own neighborhoods—police would have viciously dispersed them, very quickly. If there were clandestine black gangs their impact must have been very small.

One of these days I hope to meet George Foremen, one of my heroes. Though he is about a decade younger than me, he might be able to tell me what life in Houston's Fifth Ward was like in the 1950s. I'll bet the repression of black folks was so great that forming gangs having great impact anywhere in Houston was not possible.

Latino gang members in particular, and Latino students in general, kept to themselves. The segregation was so complete that I can remember only one Latino student from my time at Deady. Rolando, as I will call him, had a withered arm and a permanently bent leg. One day after gym class, a white student so insulted him that he was determined to fight, despite his disabilities. A crowd gathered and watched in silence as Rolando awkwardly defended himself. The boy he was fighting must have known what the on-lookers were thinking. Had he dared take advantage of Rolando he would have been in big trouble: "getting it on" with a disabled boy was as unmanly as attacking a younger and smaller boy. Soon the bully withdrew and the mostly white audience milled around Rolando, offering him compliments and pats on the back. Exceptionally admirable behavior, courageous in this case, can break down boundaries between members of relatively powerful and relatively powerless groups.

Much of oppression suffered by people of color and was undoubtedly at the hands of the Houston police. Though the sample of Houston police that I encountered directly or indirectly was small and, therefore, unrepresentative, I cannot avoid a very negative impression of Houston's "finest" during the 1950s and 1960s. An early run-in with them occurred during my "hoodlum" period. While a friend and I were running up the stairs to the movie-house balcony making as much noise as we could muster, we ran smack into an officer who immediately threw me up against the wall. He snarled as he held me there for a moment, then he reached into his pocket and extracted a switchblade knife. Aiming it at my head, he declared that he was going to cut off my "dirty" long hair and some other parts of my anatomy. I was duly frightened and promised to be quiet as a mouse thereafter. Later, one afternoon during my high school years, I saw a Houston motorcycle officer tumble off his bike into a ditch. When I approached him it was clear that he was too drunk to get up, much less drive off. In 1968, many Houston police officers placed stickers supporting racist Presidential-candidate George Wallace on their police cars and got away with it: their superiors must have condoned it. There were rumors at the time that they were regularly beating up "hippies" and civil rights workers.

During the 1970s I returned to Houston to visit old high school buddies. Several of us "went out on the town" one evening and admittedly had too much to drink. One of us, a big guy who had been a star on our football team, really "got blasted" and became belligerent. Probably because of his imposing size, the bar owner called the police. To our astonishment, not only did several police cars arrive on the scene, but a police helicopter circled the bar aiming a stoplight at us as we were ushered outside. The over-reaction was amazing ... and the problem was solved too easily. The friend was taken to the local police station. The rest of us followed. While we waited to learn our friend's fate, we struck up a conversation with one of the officers. It turned out that he had attended our high school and knew many of our classmates. As soon as he discovered "who we were" he disappeared into the interior of the station and returned with our friend in tow. Having a connection to a police officer was enough to get our friend off Scot-free. We were glad to get out of that tense situation, but I had the gut feeling that justice had not been served. I don't believe that our friend should have been jailed, or even fined—there had been no damage to the bar. However, he should have been freed after "due process" of some sort had run its course.

These tales of encounters with the Houston police may make it seem that I'm anti-police. Nothing could be further from the truth. My brother-in-law, always a close friend, has been a dedicated police officer for more than four decades. He is a man of great integrity and I believe that he exemplifies the character of most police officers. His example is one reason why one of our daughters is now a conscientious police officer who believes in and lives by the motto "to protect and serve." As to the Houston police, it should be noted that not all, or even most, Houston officers of yesteryear engaged in the despicable behavior I have described. Nevertheless, one wonders why at least some officers didn't openly deplore the bigoted and brutal behavior displayed by a substantial minority of police, especially when fellow officers were putting Wallace stickers on publicly financed police cars. Even so, it is reasonable to assume that abusive officers, like those patrolling Houston's streets during the 1950s and 1960s, are rare today. I'll bet that current Houston police officers are much more devoted to justice and fairness now than they were back then. Let those among their predecessors who behaved unjustly be remembered only as examples of how not to represent the honored profession of police officer.

During the Park Place period, other events raised my curiosity about race. One such was taking up weightlifting to help my football performance. A friend across the street and I both had sets of the old iron weights on steel bars. I worked year around and built myself up enough to gain a place on my Junior and High School teams, which would have eluded me otherwise. Being interested in physical strength I noticed the small but muscular black man working in a neighbor's yard across one of the streets that bordered our house. As we were both often doing yard work at the same time, it was natural to talk during breaks. Jack, as I will call him, was a nice guy and smart. Contrary to the stereotype "blacks are lazy," he was very hardworking, which is the rule for black people I've known. He also was a fine conversationalist who could talk about any subject that came up. I learned during our many discussions that his job across the street was only one of several he had.

During one such talk he remarked about our weightlifting and I invited him to come join us during a session. My friend and I expected that he would be very strong, because the heavy work he did gave him a lean and muscular look. To the contrary, we were astonished to find that he was rather weak. We could lift much more weight than Jack. Thinking about this observation later, I got an insight into why Jack's appearance was deceiving. Watching him work, I could see that he was exhausted. Like most black spouses and parents, he was working himself into a state of collapse just trying to keep his family afloat. He was an intelligent man who could only find employment using his hands.

On another occasion I watched with interest when a black man approached my mother in our front yard and asked for a drink of water. She told him to go around to the back door where she provided him with a glass of water. After he left, she filled a pan with water, dropped the glass in and boiled it. When I reflected on my college-educated mother later, I marveled at the fact that she could hire a black maid to handle and cook her food, do her laundry, and touch almost everything in her house while doing housework, but needed to boil the glass used by a black person. It is the kind of doublethink that characterized white people.

Another occasion that sticks out in my mind was a trip to Austin, Texas to see the Texas Aggies play the Texas Longhorns. My junior high buddies and I were great Southwest Conference football fans, and, as a group, favored the Aggies. To see the Aggies take on their biggest rival was very special. We approached our parents about attending the game, expecting they would declare us too young to make the trip. Amazingly, they let us take the train to Austin. The trip of a few hours both ways provided an opportunity to talk about anything and everything that came to mind.

A Jewish boy I'll call Albert was among those making the trip. I had known him for quite a while before I was informed by the others that he "didn't believe in Jesus," a revelation that absolutely floored me. I had never heard of anyone who didn't believe in Jesus. However, this shocking fact about Albert soon faded in importance because he was a fun guy to be with. Brighter than any one else I knew, Albert also was an excellent debater, as we all discovered on the trip to Austin.

While we argued about this and that, there was little emotion expressed until something brought up stereotypes about black people. Blacks were dirty; blacks were lazy; blacks were stupid, etc. Whatever the irrational belief, Albert adroitly reduced it to nonsense in short order. That day he taught me that many of the beliefs we harbor about people who are different from us are illogical and inconsistent with widely available facts as well as with other beliefs that we hold. Among the latter are that "all people are created equal" and "everyone has an equal chance to make it in America." I had learned in school to believe these "principles" and others like them. Yet, every day I could see that there were people who were denied an equal chance at success. I think that the discrepancy between what I was hearing from my teachers and reading in my textbooks and what I saw during everyday life led me to the conclusion that our "principles" defined the reality of some of us more than others.

I had many good teachers during my K-12 years, but a few stand out. Among them was a teacher at Deady, who later was my supervisor when I coached flag football and performed other duties at the YMCA. Gene Lightfoot was a World War II sailor whose zaniness was surpassed only by his courage in the face of danger. In class, Gene was an excellent teacher who seemed grim and humorless. Any misbehavior on the part of a male student was met with immediate physical punishment in the form of a spanking with a wooden paddle, the typical Deady schoolteacher's response to rule violations during the 1950s. He was so good with this instrument of retribution that students dubbed him "Heavyhand."

When I worked at the Y during high school and early college years, Gene would regale his young charges with tales of his World War II adventures. He was not bragging when he ruminated about his exploits during the War. Rather, he was just trying to teach some valuable lessons. For example, once he said to me, "Bem, don't ever volunteer [for dangerous, nonessential duty]." To illustrate his point he related how he had twice faced death at the behest of a Navy officer. During a training exercise an officer asked for volunteers to demonstrate tactics for escaping from beneath water that was ablaze. Oil was spread over an area of the ocean and set afire to simulate an oil spill from a torpedoed ship. Gene's hand went up fast and he readily dove into the inferno. The technique for survival was simple: you hold your breath like crazy and frantically swim underwater until you hope that you have cleared the burning water.

On another occasion, volunteers were asked to scale one of their ship's masts and climb into a lookout perch. The job was at once easy and terrifying: volunteers were to look for Japanese Kamikaze pilots who were willing to give their lives for their Emperor by crashing their planes onto the decks of US ships. Again, Gene volunteered quickly. For hours he sat in that crow's nest screaming above the din of anti-aircraft guns into a phone connected to gun stations below, vainly attempting to convey distances and locations of Kamikazes that appeared to be headed straight at him. The lesson was well learned: I've been very cautious about volunteering for non-charitable and non-essential duty ever since.

But I read too much into Gene's message. Especially in view of the stereotypes about the Japanese that I already harbored, I took the description of the Kamikazes as confirmation of the belief that there are "others" (non-whites) who are much more prone to cruelty and the perpetration of atrocities than are "we." After all, Kamikazes were as happy to crash into hospital-ships as they were to blow up on the decks of aircraft carriers. After Gene's stories inspired a fledgling interest in World War II that later became an obsession, my understanding changed. I came to believe that, in the context of war, soldiers of any stripe are subject to the commission of irrational and immoral acts. It is the nature of war that generates inhumane behavior, not the race, ethnicity or generation of the warriors. I think that we would go to war much less often if we had a better understanding of what we would be getting our young people into. But we don't want to think about it and are helped in that act of avoidance by governments that, for example, prohibit the publication of pictures showing coffins returning from battle-sites. Contrary to the anti-Vietnam-war protesters anthem "study war no more," maybe, for the sake of our survival, it is time for citizens in the USA and elsewhere to learn all we can about what war does to human thinking, emotions, and behavior. To do otherwise is to risk the reoccurrence of tragedies like the murder of innocent Iraqi civilians by US soldiers driven mad after having witnessed the dismemberment of comrades by a roadside bomb.

Gene had a certain presence, a sort of commanding appearance and a certain aura of fearlessness. He could bring order to a chaotic situation simply by directing a stern expression at those displaying unruly behavior. Being in despair over my inability to control students in the YMCA after-school program at a largely Latino school and knowing that Gene might have a solution, I appealed to him for help. The students at this school were not mean or purposefully disrespectful; they simply had not been trained to follow instructions issued by non-parental adults. During the pledge of allegiance that opened the program, these kids would, in the course of wrestling with one another, tumble all over the stage of the school auditorium and, thereby, disrespect the flag. When it came time for games, I couldn't get them organized into teams. Gene didn't tell me what to do. That wasn't his style. He came to the school with me to show me, by example, how to handle rambunctious kids.

When we arrived at the auditorium the kids were literally mopping the stage floor with their clothes as they rolled around giggling and shouting to one another. While some were in danger of falling off the stage, others were in the process of tearing down the curtains. Gene marched right up to the stage and shouted something to the effect of "stop that right now." He glared at them with his uniquely authoritative expression, and, to my amazement, they ceased their out-of-control behavior and oriented toward him as if they expected a command that would redefine the situation. They got it. He told them to line up across the stage, face the flag, and recite the pledge. They followed these instructions quickly and in good order without uttering a word. Gene then split them up into teams in preparation for the first of several games I had scheduled. After that, I did my best to mimic Gene and had no further trouble with this bunch of kids I had thought to be uncontrollable. But, even now, I still cannot explain the miracle he wrought that day. Some people have special qualities that can't be captured in words.

If Gene was stern in class, he was a cut-up elsewhere. A camp-out I attended, along with Gene and other YMCA workers in his charge, provides a good example. The freedom that comes with immersion in nature reduced Gene to an age much younger than my own at the time. He was laughing, romping through the woods, and joyfully playing the usual children's camp-games ... and also engaging in some unusual contests. As to the latter, he tried to recruit me to join him and other YMCA workers in a BB gun fight. Partly because of the "don't volunteer" lesson, and partly because I had, during the Jacinto City period, engaged in BB gun fights and received a wound under one eye, I declined. Undeterred, Gene spent most of the night firing BBs at others and being hit by their return fire. He was the first fearless, thrill-seeker I ever encountered—and I have since never met his equal—but more importantly, the combination of wacky and wise made him one of the most fascinating people I've ever known.

After graduating from Deady at mid-term, I enrolled at Milby High School in January of 1956. Milby had a very undeserved bad reputation. That the North-end and the East-end were the most economically depressed sections of Houston at least partly explains the bad rep. In the case of Milby, an East-end school, I suspect that the concentration of Latino people in the area was also a reason for the bias. In addition, white people in the East-end tended to be working class—with many fathers of students employed in the oil and chemical refineries near east Houston—whereas professional-class whites tended to live in the Southwest part of town. I was blissfully unaware of this classism until I enrolled in college and pledged a fraternity. It was clear that my pledge was accepted despite my East-end origin and that some brothers from more prosperous neighborhoods were initially standoffish, because of my more humble background.

The gangs were still another reason why the East-end was regarded with disdain. Both the North and East ends were known for their gang activity. In the North, gangs were apparently exclusively white and extremely vicious. I remember a North-end gangster named Pug Barfield who was ahead of his time. During the 1950s, Pug was stabbing people and, when he or his gang members were put on trial, threatening jurors, just as is true of some modern gangsters.

As indicated earlier, there were both white and Latino youth gangs in the East-end. Apparently people elsewhere assumed that both made it to Milby High School. If so, they were wrong. Most of the gangsters at Deady took advantage of a Texas law that allowed 16-year-olds to drop out of school. Thus, few made it to Milby and those who did were out-numbered. If they dared to bully other students, someone took them on. In one case, when a notorious Deady gangster, who enrolled at Milby, tried to bully a football player, he was so badly beaten and humiliated that he dropped out of school. East-end gangsters didn't tend to make it to high school or stay long if they did enroll. As a result, Milby was a very safe and secure place to be.

It was also an academically sound school. There were some poor teach-ers. One such, a biology instructor, spent class-time recounting his exploits as a college football player. His grading procedure was simple: pretty girls and varsity players were awarded As, while sub-varsity players and less endowed girls were given at most Bs. I was on the B football team at the time and received a B. One geometry teacher was so burned-out and apparently senile that we had to teach ourselves—I wasn't up to the task and performed badly. But for every poor teacher, there were several who were excellent. Mr. Johnson who taught algebra and trigonometry with uncommon skill and dedication, was better than my university math pro-fessors. I made Bs under his exacting standards, but, with little effort, did better in the same courses at my university. My Latin teacher, whose name escapes me now, was also outstanding. My knowledge of Latin learned in her class is still valuable to me today. Finally, an English teacher taught me to love the classic novels and a physics teacher opened my eyes to the won-ders of science. Perhaps the greatest tribute to these excellent teachers is that an uncommonly large proportion of my class went on to graduate from college, and several of us have post graduate degrees. Among our numbers are several university professors, a successful dentist who returned to his dental school as a teacher, several successful business entrepreneurs, and one the greatest basketball coaches in Texas hoop history.

The latter individual has led a remarkable life. During his late teens and early twenties, bigotry was eating away at him. As is often the case, it was making him miserable and badly affecting his personal and professional life. He had, even as a high school student and early college student, showed signs of greatness as a coach. I was his assistant in a children's park basketball-league and marveled at his ability to motivate players. But after graduating from college, he indicated that he would not consider coaching because there would surely be black players on his team.

Then he changed suddenly and dramatically. To my astonishment, being Baptized and saved made a new person of him. The hatred that is part and parcel of prejudice faded and his success as a coach developed rapidly. During his career, awards and achievements included winning his district's championship many times, making the state championship series several times, and being named Texas Basketball Coach of the Year. True to his character, when he retired recently he left the best talent he had ever developed to his assistant coach, who then ably led the team to the Texas State Championship. More importantly, he and his wife have been surrogate father and mother to many players over the years, most of them black. A remarkable proportion of them went on to attain college degrees earned on basketball scholarships, accomplishments what would have eluded them due to their disadvantaged status, had they not been the beneficiaries of his wisdom, affection and loyalty. I have often mentioned him to my students who wonder whether adult humans can radically and permanently change for the better. His life provides proof positive: yes they can.

Most of what I "recall" about Latino students is based on retrospective contemplation of personal experiences with them and on their relations with white students. During my high school years I can recall no open conflicts between white and Latino students. Nor was I aware of any undercurrents of discord. Unlike at Deady where the distance between white and Latino students was only slightly, and mostly temporarily, moderated by incidents like that involving Rolando, a casual observer of students at Milby during the mid to late 1950s might have concluded that there were no barriers between white and Latino students and that intermingling between the two groups was common. In fact, it was possible for some Latino students to be widely admired by white students.

One case in point was a young man who was good at everything. Carlos, as I will call him, was an A student and a prominent member of the Academic Honor Society. He also was a four-sport letterman and the very capable backup quarterback on the football team. In addition, he was a handsome, congenial, and likable person. Carlos was often praised but I can recall no disparaging comments about him. Thus, he was another exception. Accordingly, though interracial dating was tacitly disapproved by whites and Latinos at Milby, and almost never occurred, there was barely a lifting of eyebrows when Carlos began to date a white girl.

Another exception was an outstanding football player. I'll call him Alberto. Those who watched interactions among players during practices or during games probably would have concluded that there was complete acceptance of Latino players on the part of white players. Consistent with the claim of most sports fans, it would have appeared that it is how well you play the game and whether you are a "team player" that mattered, not your sources of identity. Alberto was widely admired. Everyone was happy to hang out with him on the practice field or in the halls between classes. But what about when the three o'clock bell rings or, during football season, when practice was over?

I can remember wanting to be known as a friend of an outstanding white player two class levels ahead of me who went on to play at the University of Texas. It didn't happen outside the school setting, but it might have: he knew my sister and many of her friends. At the time I must have non-consciously sensed that being Alberto's friend was also not going to happen, but for different reasons than in the case of the white star-player. Partly in retrospect, it is now clear to me that white and Latino students did not interact after the bell rang or the practice was over. There are degrees of segregation and it may be that in today's "integrated" schools this more subtle form of segregation prevails.

Further, not only does subtle (and not so subtle) segregation go unchallenged by the various racial and ethnic groups, it may also be implicitly endorsed by those groups' members. Sadly, in recent years there is a drift back to the old form of overt segregation—all black, all white, and all Latino schools. This trend has increased following the peak of school integration attained during the early 1990s. Allegedly, students, often acting at the behest of their parents, are willfully sorting themselves into schools populated by "their own kind." Today, Milby is 93% Latino, with blacks constituting 5% of students, Whites 1% and Asians less than 1% (statistics from Milby's web page). As always, it is an academically sound school with excellent sports programs.

Again, because black people were largely confined to the third, fourth, and fifth wards of Houston, they were invisible to most whites. Thus, there are very few significant incidents involving blacks and whites that I can recall from my high school years. However, one incident does stick out as a good example of mean-spiritedness directed toward blacks. Although I don't recall who related the incident in question, I do have a very clear memory of it. One of my fellow students told how he and a friend drove through the streets of Houston at cruise speed in search of black pedestrians. When a suitable target was located, he was approached from behind at such a slow speed that the car engine could barely be heard. Once a black, male target was along side the car, one of its occupants threw the contents of a milk-shake-cup at the unsuspecting man and shouted "acid." The act, so boldly recounted, ended in cowardice as the car sped away with its horn honking and its tires spinning. The kid who related the story laughed uproariously as he mimicked the black man's horrified look and frantic attempts to wipe the frozen concoction off his body. Add cruelty to sex and aggression as the only themes of jokes that inspire laughter in too many people.

Except for Latinos, non-white and non-Christian students were rare at Milby. I remember children of only one Jewish family who attended Milby (the Jewish boy I knew at Deady had moved away). The father of the family had a small general store that included tomato plants among its stock. As we had a greenhouse in Park Place, a friend and I grew tomato plants and sold them to the father. Our plants were pretty pathetic and he often grumbled as he paid us, but he continued to support our enterprise out of kindness, though I'm sure he lost on the deal.

There was also one American Indian family and one Indian coach. A boy and a girl from the Indian family were my classmates. She was one of the most beautiful girls in the school, and that wasn't just my opinion: there were annual "Most Beautiful" and "Most Handsome" contests for each grade. By the time I was a senior I dated a few girls regularly, though I mostly asked out different girls each week, but I never asked out the "Most Beautiful." They were out of my league.

Her brother was a member of the football team. He was not a great athlete, but totally fearless, a "hard hitter." That he was Indian was acknowledged by a teammate, known for his humorous quips, who speculated on how our huddle must have looked from the stands and to our opponents. He said that just before the huddle broke, observers would see a hand holding a tomahawk thrusting upward out of the middle of the clustered players. We all laughed and would never have predicted that some Indians would be offended by it today.

Our Indian coach was a very short, bald man with rounded shoulders and leathery, ruddy skin hanging from an aging frame. His rubbery face was typically formed into a fearsome scowl, but it changed dramatically when he let loose with his patented, thunderous laugh, usually in response to some stupid behavior on the part of a player. Coach Samuel, as I will call him, was noted for frequent displays of bad temper. Players who had been on the team several years before I joined told scary tales about him. Allegedly, before practice, he would work his way into a state of ultimate meanness by practicing his scowl in a dressing room mirror. Supposedly, during practices he cursed players and kicked them in the butt when they lay too long on the ground after being knocked down. When players made mistakes a hard slap to the side of their plastic helmets rang their ears and rattled their brains.

He must have gotten in trouble for this abusive behavior because, by the time I played, he said and did very little except to occasionally curse an errant player. I was told that he admired only "gutsy" players. His model player was said to be a guy who was so sick during a game that he was throwing up while running after opposing players, but he refused to be taken out. Though mean and intelligent don't seem to go together, coach

Samuel was very bright. He not only had graduated from college but he also had an advanced degree in science. These three American Indians constituted the sole sources of my knowledge about Indians. So, if I were asked, "beautiful, violent, mean and smart" was what I could say about Indians. Many years later, I learned that American Indians display great diversity along many dimensions, just as is true of any group numbering in the millions.

Of course, there were no black coaches back then, but the times were sure to change. When I was in college I returned to Milby to visit our football line-coach who had become head coach. In an exasperated tone, he told me about how so much had changed for the worse. Now, he said, boys in his gym classes actually talked back to him. During my time at Milby, that would have been extremely unlikely behavior on the part of a male student (female students rarely committed serious infractions). Then, misbehaving male students would have been severely paddled, but the practice had been outlawed because of complaints from students' parents. How he must have longed for the good old days. Though I don't condone physical punishment of students at any educational level, I'll admit that I've occasionally become nostalgic for "the good old days."

On the same occasion, he introduced me to his black assistant coach. With a straight face he related that they got along well because, "I said I wouldn't call him a 'nigger' if he wouldn't call me a 'honky'." The black coach smiled nervously. As he was the only black person I saw that day, I'm sure that he knew that he was terribly outnumbered. Although my ex-coach's comments were less than endearing, they don't diminish him in my mind. He was a very good man in most respects.

In relating this incident, I've made an exception to a practice I've followed for many years: I don't speak or spell out the n-word. One reason the exception was made here is a compelling comment by daughter Kathleen. She suggested that the impact of a revered figure uttering the n-word is diminished by not spelling it out. Another reason for the exception is that it provides an opportunity to examine why the n-word has become so controversial. A recent front-page article in the Peoria Journal Star (PJS; 1/7/2007) explored reasons why the n-word is still in use and why that fact is debated in both the black and white communities. The article quotes a key line from black Harvard law professor Randall Kennedy's 2001 book entitled "N....: The Strange Career of a Troublesome Word": "[the n-word has provided] the sound track to American racism." And yet, Kennedy has defended the free use of the word in court, including serving as lawyer for a white man who used the word while beating a black man with a baseball bat. As everyone knows, some black entertainers continue to use the word and white Seinfeld co-star, Michael Richards (Kramer), used it loudly and repeatedly when black members of his audience voiced their disdain for his comedic performance. But why should it and its variations ("nigga," a supposed "term of endearment" used by one black person in reference to another, and wigger, a white wannabe) not be used? It continues to be uttered with relish by racists such as Neo-Nazis and Ku Klux Klan members and has been used by white people with power over the lives of black people, for example, Presidents Abraham Lincoln, Harry Truman and Lyndon Johnson. It has also appeared on products sold in the USA throughout the 1880s and for much of the 1900s. Not covered in the PJS is the fact that use of the n-word, or words related to it, is hotly debated in Asia and elsewhere. Because it's a small world and getting smaller, international variants of the n-word may be leaking into the lexicon of the USA. Senator George Allen (no relation) may have lost his seat in the Senate, because he publicly called a person of color a "macaca," a derogatory word of uncertain origin that is considered a racial slur in some parts of the Asia, Europe and Africa. However, number one on my list of reasons for not using the n-word is that it was the last insult to the ears of many black men (and women) before the Klan hangman's noose snuffed out their lives. I think that the word should not be used by anyone, and I don't care if that conclusion gets me accused of "political correctness," a well-intentioned, badly implemented, nearly dead movement.

Reflecting back on myself during the Milby years is painful. I didn't like myself back then and I still don't like myself as I think about who I was at that time. Because of my training in psychology it has become clear to me that I was unknowingly depressed. Like many teens I didn't understand the negative emotions that I directed to myself. As a result I was mired in self-pity because of all of my imagined shortcomings. I spent most of my time feeling sorry for myself. On the football field, at times I was nearly suicidal, willing to break my limbs, or someone else's, in order to earn a spot on the starting team. At other times, I backed off, playing just hard enough to get by.

Religion became the refuge from my troubles. Though I was serious about it only during my teens, my exposure to religion dates to infancy. Mama claimed that I selected the Episcopal Church for our family. Supposedly, when I was a baby, the Episcopal service was the only one during which I could sit until the end without crying more loudly than the minister preached (here I used "minister," as Mama preferred it; elsewhere I use "priest"; both are acceptable). Unfortunately, Mama often resorted to confabulation in order to reshape her reality to fit her pre-conceptions and needs. Thus, her apocryphal story about my selection of the Episcopal Church may be taken as seriously as her tale about how I developed curly hair. Rather than attributing my curls to my genes, she believed that a woolen cap she placed on my infantile head had turned my straight hair into ringlets.

When I was a preteen, I served as an acolyte, more to placate my parents than to "be religious." However, by the time I was in high school I became "a devout Christian." My friends knew that I attended services every Sunday and participated by lighting and extinguishing the candles as well as assisting the priest with the communion ceremony (the best part of which was drinking the unused wine, among my first experiences with alcohol). During my last years in high school, I became an acolyte manager whose duty it was to teach boys the acolyte's role during Sunday services. In this capacity, I spent a number of hours during the week teaching neophyte acolytes how to carry the processional cross, be silent and sit up straight during the services, look pious, and be highly deferent in the presence of the priest. So I was being what a good person should be. I was "doing the right thing" from the point of view of many of my friends and many adults, but I was doing it for the wrong reasons. I wanted to look good and be pure to counteract my underlying feelings of worthlessness. Being religious was merely a means to that end.

My righteousness sometimes lapsed into self-righteousness, which generated a serious conflict with grandmother Polly. Polly didn't go to church. She believed that "God is everywhere ... you don't need to go to church to find him." To her, one communicates with God in private motivated only by a desire for a personal relationship with the Almighty. She thought that people who go to church to pray in public are too often ostentatious and sanctimonious in their approach to religion. I disagreed vehemently, probably because her beliefs threatened my own. On one occasion I became so upset that I followed her to her bedroom door arguing my "go to church" point of view. She slipped inside and firmly shut the door. It wouldn't be the last time she shut the door in my face.

When I look back at this period, I'm amazed that my friends stuck with me. Some of them knew of my state—they would make comments like "quit worrying about yourself all the time"—but supported me anyway. One prime example occurred after a football game during which I committed several holding fouls resulting in penalties that were a factor in our defeat. While I cried in the corner of the dressing room lamenting my several "stupid mistakes," teammates who were brought low by a defeat that was another nail in the coffin of our playoff hopes, put aside their own misery and came by to comfort me. Sometimes I wonder whether what I needed at the time was more a swift kick to the gluteus maximus than a lot of sympathy (I imagine there were at least a few of my classmates who would have accommodated this need). But here is one thing I'm sure about: it is doubtful that I would have made it out of my high school years were it not for such good and true friends. We still get together for class reunions and other events at least every five years.

As I reflect back on my youth, another source of amazement is that, although my memories of experiences with race are startlingly vivid today, I understood so little about the racial incidents I observed back then. After reading a draft of this book, daughter Margaret wanted to know what I felt and thought about, for example, as I observed my mother boiling the water glass used by a black man. To this day, I see my childhood and adolescent self as sensing that something significant had happened concerning race, but having no clue about what to make of the racially-charged incidents I observed. Regarding my youth more generally, I sometimes remark to friends and family, "I didn't have a thought worth thinking until I entered college." It was as if I was merely recording what happened. If so, it was not necessarily an empty exercise. Perhaps I was collecting gems that I could not evaluate until maturity gave me a microscope to put them under. That is a reason why early memories are precious: We can sometimes dredge them up and render them meaningful for the first time. But a word of caution is in order. As Alfred Adler recognized more than 70 years ago, and modern memory researchers have confirmed today, our early (and recent) memories my be vividly recalled, and we may be certain about them, but we may be wrong.

4

Undergraduate Years

Upon entering college, for the first time, my mind became fully functional, and I began to think productively about issues in my life and, more importantly, about broad concerns beyond myself. The woes of my high school days were replaced with feelings of joy at having some understanding of my existence. I became a different person, though I would not have met many people's criteria for having attained "better person" status.

Though I became a psychology major, I took more philosophy than psych courses. Classes in epistemology, philosophy of science, and history of philosophy—several of which included discussions of religion—began what could be called my cynical period. Reflecting on my teen years, I recalled some incidents that meshed with my new questioning mode. In one such occurrence, a big and brutish priest took pleasure in mashing boys against gym walls during pick-up basketball games at church functions. In another case, a priest who was funny, interesting and intellectually open was fired on the basis of mere rumors that he was having an affair with his secretary.

By the time I was a sophomore, I had renounced religion calling it the refuge of hypocrites. Years later I discovered that I had never genuinely embraced it. To this day I'm struggling to understand religion and spirituality. All that I can say for sure is that I respect people who embrace religion for reasons of deep and genuine faith, rather than to accommodate ulterior motives.

I had a heck of a lot of fun in college doing the things that college students still do. However, when I see my behavior as a college student displayed by students enrolled in my classes during the late 1960s to the mid 2000s, my own deportment doesn't look so good. Maybe college students do what they do, and fail to do what they should, because they know in the backs of their minds that only four years down the road they will face what may appear to be a stark and unforgiving reality, accompanied by burdensome responsibilities.

As my high school friends had dispersed to various colleges and careers, I needed a new source of belonging. Thus, after a first semester as a part-time student at the University of Houston, I joined a fraternity. The desire to be a part of a group sustained me through the demeaning and pointless pledge period. The fraternity had periodic "rallies" during which pledges were harassed—sometimes physically—and humiliated. For example, we were sent on a scavenger hunt that led one of us to crawl into the elephant pen at the Houston zoo and retrieve some pachyderm feces, some of which each of us placed into our pants-pockets for the duration of "Hell Week." Even after years of teaching about social conformity, I still can't believe I did that. On "hell night," the last night of the week, we were attired in women's dresses, placed in the back of a pickup truck during the dead of winter, and driven to a forest stream into which we were told to dive. It was the coldest night of my life. On the way back to the fraternity house I was forced to drink some obnoxious stuff which made me so violently ill that I regurgitated all over the back seat of my Big Brother's car. All of this was supposed to make us appreciate the fraternity and commit to it. The logic was "if you suffer for something you will learn to love it." I did come to love my fraternity, but it was in spite of the macho games that constituted the semester of pledging, not because of it.

During one of these Hell Week rallies I became dehydrated and asked for a drink. Not surprisingly, I was offered a beer. I drank it rapidly and enjoyed the buzz. In retrospect my behavior was remarkable as it was my first alcoholic drink since my hoodlum days (not counting the communion wine mixed with water) and represented a sudden and complete abandonment of the self-denial that characterized me in high school. While at Milby I eschewed even a soda—it was bad for my conditioning—much less accept an alcoholic drink—drinking was sinful.

Fraternity activities haven't changed very much except that, just as gangs have "progressed" from knives to automatic weapons, Greeks of today—college students more generally—apparently are doing everything we did but they carry it to greater extremes.

Conversations around my fraternity house were confined largely to women, booze, and sports. I was into all three pursuits. We partied every weekend and inevitably at least some of us got drunk. Sometimes I was among the inebriated. Apparently, it appears that students, beginning in the 1970s and with increasing likelihood up to the present time, are starting to "party" (euphemistic for getting drunk) by the middle of the week.

Our usual party involved bringing a date to the frat house where a band of black musicians played mainly what I called the "funeral dirge." They might start with some rousing music to which we did the "whip" and other holdovers from the boogie days. However, the music got slower after every break taken by the band until it seemed that the sounds were coming from an old crank-powered phonograph that was in need of a re-wind. Of course, the band could drink as much as they wanted, but, while we drank mainly beer, sometimes consuming three kegs by the end of the festivities, they often brought hard liquor. So did some brothers. As the evening wore on, that band-members eyes became glazed over was apparent to us, even as we missed the fact that our eyes were similarly affected. Neither did we notice that we had slowed down at least as much as the band.

Rumor had it that the progressive deterioration of the band was more due to hard drug use than to liquor consumption. Some brothers even claimed to have seen needle marks on band members' arms. So you'd think we would never hire them again. In fact, we tended to stick with a given band until they were no longer available. "They" came cheap. And if they used drugs, so what? It was considered the norm for "them."

A second kind of party was more about getting laid. These were joint fraternity and sorority parties where the women came to our house and nobody brought dates. Although the total people present rarely exceeded fifty, it was at these parties that we emptied the greatest number of beer kegs. We believed in the motto, "candy and flowers is kinder, but liquor is quicker." By early the next morning, most people left alone, but the "lucky" ones paired up. At the next weekly fraternity meeting—usually the Sunday after the Saturday night party—those who did take a drunken woman home invariably described in excruciating detail the sex they alleg-edly had. Some braggarts were believed more than others, but each had a willing audience.

That there was anything wrong with this behavior never seemed to occur to any of us, even when the moral implications should have been obvious. In one extreme case a sister in a sorority attending a party at our house was "gang-banged" in one of the brother's cars parked outside. She was described as dead drunk and, in retrospect, the words they used to characterize her made her seem very depressed. Later, grist from the rumor mill made it appear that self-loathing led her to that car that night. What-ever her reasons might have been, given that she had a reason or was able to reason at all, she was used by a few of my fraternity brothers, who later described the incident in an indifferent tone, devoid of any signs of remorse. Her sorority sisters found out about the incident and reacted by dismissing her from the sorority. As for me, I can recall only puzzlement: why did they do that? Although my classes were beginning to make me conscious of racial injustice, it would be a long time before I began to develop any meaningful sensitivity to the exploitation of women that con-tinues to be an international crisis today.

As I write about this incident I understand that it might be interpreted as a condemnation of fraternities. It is not so intended. This kind of behavior no more characterized my fraternity brothers as a group than it would any other group of men existing then or today. Most of them were truly fine people who I continue to respect and admire. Sadly, however, the behavior of a few fraternity men "back in the day" is still condoned by some men in this supposedly "more enlightened" era. As for my particular fraternity, it was one of the first, if not the first, to develop a mandatory program for all chapters devoted to teaching respect for women and to condemn any form of coerced sex.

Harsh hazing of pledges became a source of division in our fraternity. I was probably the leader of the anti-hazing faction. When an election for fraternity President was held during my senior year, my name was placed on the ballot and I won. Those of us who opposed mistreatment of pledges passed a resolution declaring that drunkenness during pledge rallies was not to be tolerated and that no member was to touch a pledge during a rally, much less physically abuse him.

Unfortunately, as is true of most groups of college students, our ranks included some alcoholics. These individuals could not refrain from drinking at any fraternity function. Thus, it was unsurprising that at the first rally following the passage of the resolution, a habitual drunk showed up inebriated, angry, and out of control. Before several brothers could intervene, this pathetic individual punched a pledge, kicked him, and was proceeding to beat up his victim.

It was a particularly sorry scene as pledges were told in no uncertain terms that they were never to talk back to a member, and certainly not to respond in a physical way to anything said about them or done to them by a member. Obviously, pledges were helpless and attacking them was an act of cowardice. Such behavior was dishonorable in a fraternity where "honor" was the key word in the liturgy read at every meeting. Accordingly, I thought that suspending this abusive drunk would be widely accepted and would serve as a warning to would-be abusers.

I was dead wrong. The suspension of the abuser made the ideological split in our ranks became a crevasse so wide and deep that it appeared impossible to bridge. There were rumors that I would be removed from office unless I accepted hazing and reinstated the abuser. Not knowing what else to do, I bluffed. Before the next meeting I was pointedly threatened with impeachment as I approached the house. I was able to get the meeting started and after the opening ritual I immediately issued my own threat. Those present were reminded that hazing of pledges was against our fraternity's laws and I planned to notify our national office about the incident at our chapter. While I knew that hazing was prohibited, I also knew that it was so commonly practiced the national office had to know it was going on. Would representatives at the national office support me? Some of those who shared my feelings about hazing thought that the national office would turn a blind eye to evidence of hazing.

But the bluff worked ... sort of. After a heated discussion laced with profanity and punctuated by fists thrust in the air, a compromise was reached. The suspension would continue in force for the remainder of the semester. However, rallies would continue, though physical harassment would be disallowed and drunken members would be forced to leave.

My hopes that this contentious meeting would be the beginning of the end of hazing in our fraternity were dashed soon after I left office and graduated. The fraternity administration that followed my own reinstated hazing and ignored the rule about drunkenness at pledge rallies. Obviously my efforts amounted to little of nothing, but there may have been some residual affect. Several years later a member informed me that hazing had finally ended and, in fact, rallies were no longer held.

Fraternity hazing continues to be a problem today. As a woman student informed me a few years ago hazing also occurs in sororities. The more modern form that has recently been in the news is forcing pledges to drink until they pass out. In several widely publicized cases, pledges have died of alcohol poisoning. I have continued to wonder what motivates such brutal behavior on the part of our society's elite: college students. One explanation that has occurred to me is that the same mean-spirited mentality that promotes the oppression of the disenfranchised in our society also is responsible for the abuse of pledges made powerless by their desire to belong. Kicking people when they are down was literally practiced by Southern police officers and Ku Klux Klan members during, and, of course, long before the civil rights era of the 1950s and 1960s.

A less metaphorical interpretation involves the observation that fraternities are infused with military tradition. Many, if not most, fraternities originated in Confederate states during the post-Civil War period. Some, including my own, were founded at military schools. Such being the case, it should not be surprising that pledge training mimicked military training. What has escaped many fraternity members over time is that, while it makes sense to train military personnel for battle, using the same methods on would-be fraternity members is nonsensical.

As for my own fraternity chapter, the military under-pinnings were obvious. The predecessor of our nationally-affiliated chapter was populated by Korean War veterans. War grows a tough hide on many of those who fight. The veterans who founded our chapter were a hard and riotous bunch. They were also fascinating. I was a receptive audience when they talked about their exploits during the war and after returning from Korea. To all of us who were just out of our teens, they seemed to be the "real men" we wanted to become.

It was well known that the vets were physically harsh during pledge training. In fact, they were accepted into our respected national fraternity despite an incident that made newspaper headlines. Just before they applied to the national fraternity, one of their pledges nearly died of exposure during a winter Hell Night. It appears that this shameful incident only moderated the ill treatment of pledges that occurred after the fraternity went national. At the same time, it may have ensured that harsh pledge training would be the policy of the new national-affiliated chapter.

Race was rarely a matter of discussion during my fraternity years. Some of my brothers did know about my point of view regarding racial discrimination. Most of them respected my position, but some of them found opportunities to argue with me about it. However, because the University of Houston was an "all-white school" until well into the 1960s, pledging blacks students was not an issue (a few foreign and Latino students were the only students of color on campus). Even when, much to its credit, the University of Houston became the first traditionally-white, Confederate-state university to recruit black athletes, their numbers were small initially and athletes tended not to pledge fraternities (currently the University of Houston is one of the most completely integrated colleges or universities in the USA).

By the 1960s, there were enough Latino students on campus for some to take part in "rush," the periodic pledge recruitment campaign. When the possibility that some of them might attempt to pledge our fraternity was discussed at meetings, a few of my brothers who hailed from towns on the Texas-Mexico border swore that they would resign from the fraternity if we initiated a "Messcan." We did pledge a Latino student, but he may have sensed the hostility of brothers from near the border. Whatever the reason, he withdrew before completing pledge training. Perhaps it was fortunate that no black students came through rush. They would have faced a hostile atmosphere. For example, as was true of most fraternities at the time, some of the bawdy drinking-ditties sung off-tune around the beer kegs were openly racist. Maybe it was paranoia, but I sometimes imagined that these songs were sung more often at parties that I attended than when I was absent.

A few years before I became President, two brothers and I made a pilgrimage to our fraternity's national meeting. Once at the meeting I went looking for brothers who also opposed the "bias clause" in the fraternity's constitution. The clause excluded blacks and Asians from membership, but not Jews several of whom were prominent in the fraternity's history. I found the president of a chapter at a Big Ten school who had actively opposed the bias clause. Together, we sought an official of the fraternity who would talk to us about the clause. We were directed to the Convention Organizer who was fresh out of college. In the course of huddling with this young fraternity official we learned that he was quite sympathetic regarding our desire to eliminate the bias clause. However, he assured us that while there was a way around the clause, it could not be eliminated. He indicated that several mostly Northern chapters of the fraternity had applied and been granted a "waiver with honor" allowing them to pledge and initiate anyone they wanted to call "brother." When we asked why resort to this "end run," he explained that most of the fraternity's chapters were in the South and most of those had indicated that they would leave the fraternity if the bias clause was eliminated. That would mean that a majority of the chapters would leave the fraternity leading to its collapse. He went on to say that he would do all he could in the future to get rid of the clause.

It was not an empty gesture. The same young man worked his way up the hierarchy of my fraternity's national office and eventually became it Chief Executive Officer. Sometime before or after he rose to CEO, the clause was eliminated. Today my fraternity has black members; at least one is a public figure and one is on the board of regents. However, examination of chapter pictures in the fraternity magazine indicates that blacks constitute a very small minority of members. This small proportion of black people in my fraternity makes it representative of traditionally white fraternities and sororities, almost all of which have only a few black members. Further, the sorry state of integration in today's sororities and fraternities is also true of their black counterparts.

In a sense, segregated fraternities and sororities are a symptom of a continuing problem in US society. As is the case with the re-segregation of our public schools, whites, blacks, and in increasing numbers, Latino students and their parents are claiming that they are "more comfortable" with "their own kind." In the case of fraternities and sororities this rationalization is supplemented by overt pressure on black and white students to pledge only black and white fraternities and sororities, respectively. White students who attempt to pledge black fraternities and sororities are likely to be regarded as "wannabes" by white and black students. Black students pledging whites fraternities and sororities are subjected to the taunts "Uncle Tom" and "sell out" by other black students. There are some reasonable arguments which convincingly assert that blacks should, for their own good and that of other black students, pledge and thereby support black fraternities, sororities and other black organizations. Members of white sororities and fraternity sometimes disingenuously invoke these arguments to justify not actively recruiting black students. The dilemma created by these pressures asserted on black and white students is the same as that implied earlier: students who, throughout their education, seek the "comfort and convenience" of being almost exclusively with "their own kind" are going to be stressed-out and handicapped when they enter the work-a-day world where they must interact smoothly with *all kinds* of people, if they hope to succeed.

Confrontations revolving around issues of race were not confined to the fraternity convention. Race reared its consternating head both before we arrived at the convention and after it was over. The two guys who accompanied me on the trip knew my point of view, didn't share it, and took great pleasure in taunting me about it. For example, as we drove to the convention from Houston to the southeastern coast of the country, we encountered many scenes that inspired comments about race. Once, while driving through some Southern state, we passed what appeared to be an antebellum plantation home, complete with a long tree-lined drive to the front door and huge, white columns supporting an overhanging roof that formed a grand front porch. My two brothers who were alone in the front seat began a discussion about how wonderful it would have been to own such a house and the slaves that went with it. While making no attempt to include me in the discussion, they ruminated on the pleasures of a leisurely life with all needs being met by obedient slaves. Slumped in the back seat, I fumed in silence biding my time until there was an opportunity to turn the tables.

After the convention we headed for New York City where we were to stay at the house of a brother we met at the convention. I had heard that trees didn't grow in Brooklyn and had expected that it would be run down. To my surprise the brother, whose father was a successful physician, lived on a charming tree-lined street in a large and comfortable house.

Our host's parents were gracious in a rather formal and superficial way. It didn't take long to learn that their basic motivation was to impress us with their affluence and "good taste." We were shown an impressive art collection that was described in such a way as to leave no doubt about the rarity and great value of each item.

I noticed a black maid working in the kitchen and, because I must have seemed curious about her, our host described the family's relationship with her. Although I could detect no affection in his voice, I inferred from what he said about her that she was viewed as a human being, if not "part of the family." Domestics described in this way are often live-in maids, but she used public transportation to get from Harlem to the Brooklyn each morning and back to Harlem in the evening. Regardless of the weather, it was her problem to get from the station to our fraternity brother's house.

With growing interest, I watched the family's interaction with her. They seemed never to speak to her except to issue orders. She kept her head down in their presence and rarely spoke except to say "Yes'um" or "Yessir." Contrary to their earlier proclamations regarding their maid, apparently the family actually viewed her only as a servant and she saw them only as her bosses. Outside the home there was no relationship. She might as well have been a robot. I was reminded of how my parents and grandmother related to their black maids.

Our host, like many long-time New York City residents, claimed to know and love all of the Big Apple's attractions. He was anxious to take us on a tour of some of the city's most famous landmarks. One of the first stops was Coney Island. I can remember nothing about our visit there except what happened when we left the park. An incredible scene played out across the street from the park entrance. A police officer with a Billy Club was racing madly down the sidewalk, steadily gaining on a dark-skinned, young man. Within a few seconds the officer was close enough to his target to deliver a blow to the back of his head that sent him sprawling to the concrete. Though it was obvious that the now bloodied man was subdued, the officer continued to pound on various parts of his body until he was no longer moving. I must have looked as horrified as I felt. Some-one standing nearby may have been trying to relieve my distress when he mumbled, "He ain't nothing but a *greaser*." I discovered before I left the city that the epithet was too often the way white New Yorkers referred to Puerto Ricans. Looking around at the crowd of on-lookers, it was clear that I had just witnessed a common occurrence about which no one cared.

Our host also insisted that we visit Harlem. We toured the world-renowned black community in his late model Lincoln Continental con-vertible with the top down. As we roamed the area, black people on the street seemed not to notice us. Apparently seeing white people slumming their neighborhood in luxurious cars was a common occurrence. Suddenly our host noted with exaggerated alarm that it was dusk and soon would be dark. After gasping that the car was low on gas, he yelled over the engine and street noise, "We got to get out of here before dark ... they'll mug us." I was genuinely frightened and I believe that my two companions on the trip were also. But as I reviewed the event that night, in my mind's eye I could see the faint smile on our host's face as he sounded his verbal alarms. He was messing with us.

On the way back to Houston, I slouched in the back seat waiting for an opportunity to retaliate for the harassment I received on the trip to the convention. We talked about all that had happened on the trip. My frater-nity brothers couldn't have been happier about almost everything we had seen and done (they didn't know that I and a fellow dissident had talked about the bias clause with the man who would eventually lead the national fraternity). I responded to their enthusiastic endorsement of almost every aspect of our trip with some mild comments. Eventually they got around to our stay in Brooklyn and the tour of New York, City. Their monumental gratitude to our host and his family gave new meaning to the word "hyperbole." Our host and his family were such fine and proper people. They had opened up their house to us and made us feel we had been adopted. Both went on and on about the beautiful house, the fine furniture, the impressive art collection, the magnificent automobile, and the generally high-class life style.

It was clear to me that these people were living the life my brothers wanted for themselves. I had found the nerve, and I hit it hard. Our host and his family were not gracious and generous. They were vulgar and ostentatious materialists, hypocrites who only pretended that they saw their maid as a genuine human being, bigots whose racism was pushed out of mind so they could make the best of it without being accountable for it. The young man of the house reflected the latter when he played on our own prejudices in order to get a strong emotional reaction out of us. As I spewed out this venom, I raised my voice to drown out their protests. It ended in expletives hurled at me and bounced back at them.

I felt good. I had gotten revenge, but it didn't take me long to realize that my behavior toward my fraternity brothers was just as deplorable as the way they had treated me. Years of teaching human cultural diversity has taught me that there are more effective and gentle ways to confront people's destructive beliefs.

While the events of the trip to the convention and to New York City are accurate within the limits of human memory, my depiction of my two fraternity brothers does not characterize them. I showed only a bad side of them, one that is shared by most white people, including myself, in order to tell a tale consistent with the theme of this book. I continue to like, respect, and admire these two brothers for all of their good qualities that far outnumber the bad ones.

It was not long after this trip that I was elected President of my fraternity. I soon discovered achieving the highest office does have its perks. We crowned a "Sweetheart" at each annual, formal ball. One day while lounging around the Cougar Den—the University Union hangout—a Sweetheart candidate tried to impress me by bragging that she could get me a date with any woman in the place. I looked around, saw a beautiful woman and said simply, "How about her?" To my pleasant surprise, she brought my choice over, introduced us and we set up a date. About a year later we were "pinned" (she wore my fraternity pin) and after about another year, we were engaged. We married three years after we were introduced. Paula and I have been together for more than forty wonderful years. We are best friends and always have been. Though thick and thin—and there were some lean times—we have been blessed. She is the life preserver that keeps me afloat and the anchor that keeps me from drifting.

Except for one semester during my sophomore year, I lived at home. During that one semester, I dwelled at the fraternity house amid the rats and roaches (I had only suspected the presence of rats until they razed the house and found a huge rat-skeleton in the attic above where I slept—finally I knew for sure about the source of the constant scratching and squeaking). After I met Paula during my senior year, I "lived" mostly at her house. Much to Mama's irritation, I came home at around 2:00 AM most nights after having had supper at my future in-laws and spending the evening watching TV with Paula. Mama acted as if I were "living off her" without being attentive to her. But she never expressed these reflections on our relationship. She was, as always, stoic. In reaction, I was distant and, frankly, insensitive. Mama didn't know about Paula until "it was serious." Nor did she know much about me. We were icebergs floating in close proximity and colliding when the winds of resentment were blowing strong. Never was there enough warmth between us to melt through the frigid protective armor down to underlying, genuine feelings. I blamed her, but it was more my fault.

Polly continued to live with Mama and Daddy throughout my junior high, high school, and college years. She was always the grand dame, emerging from her room each morning impeccably coiffured, expertly made-up, and dressed appropriately for the church services she never attended. In fact, we never saw her in any other condition. On her days off and during holidays, whenever her door opened, she stepped out "dressed up fit to kill."

Polly had her moment of Andy Warhol fame. Once she was featured in a Houston Chronicle article about one of her welfare clients whose rare disease could cause broken bones during simple acts such as walking across a room. The article portrayed her as knowledgeable, kind and patient during her efforts to help her client deal with his devastating disease. These qualities characterized her dealings with people in most spheres of her life. Polly handled her brief time in the spotlight with self-effacing equanimity. When asked about the article, she diverted the focus from herself to her client.

Polly also had her embarrassing moment on the 6 o'clock news. This upsetting public event revealed one of her prime traits: she did not suffer indignities well. During one of Houston's infamous flash floods, she ran off the road into a deep drainage ditch and had to be unceremoniously dragged from her sinking car, clothes and hair all askew. The news video showed her dripping wet and camera shy. When asked about the incident she would attempt to change the subject or, if that failed, flee to her room.

5

Graduate School

In 1963, I entered graduate school at the University of Houston choosing experimental psychology as my general area and social/personality as my specific emphasis. I took a few courses in the spring, but started in earnest during school year 1963–1964. The first year has traditionally been intellectual boot camp. Acting under the assumption that new graduate students learned nothing during undergraduate training, all the basic areas of psychology are covered in one year, six weeks at a time. Paula and I spent that year in various libraries: the U of H library, the Rice University library because it is a pleasant place to study, and the University of Texas Medical School library where I could readily find books and journals containing information about biological and neurological issues relating to psychology. If you made an "A" or a "B" in all sections, you did not have to take the preliminary exam at the end of the spring semester. I had to take the test for one section and passed it. That first grueling year was good for only one thing, as far as I was concerned: Paula and I spent most of each day together and became very close. By the end of the year, that we would get married became self-evident to both of us.

Of the 40 students across several different emphasis areas who began the program with me, only 7 of us completed our Ph.D. requirements. The first year took a heavy toll. Most of those who dropped out just couldn't keep up. Attrition thereafter was mainly due to lack of initiative. Very few students dropped out because of poor grades. Most of those who left the program couldn't deal with the lack of structure whereby they had to come up with masters thesis and dissertation topics, coax faculty members to be on their committees, recruit research participants, collect data, do statistical analyses, and, most importantly, write up the results, all of which they had to do basically on their own. A few others couldn't deal with the terror experienced during the fifth or sixth year of the program generated by the final comprehensive exam. This gigantic exam was over the current literature covering several self-selected areas (for example, developmental psychology, in my case) and some required areas (for example, statistics).

There were no people of color among the 40 students who began the program. The gender make-up of the class was about 75% male and 25% female. When it became time to consider topics under the rubric "prejudice" there were no students who could or would comment about personal experiences of discrimination. Somehow we had to glean from the dry, scientific writing of journal-research articles and graduate textbooks what life was like for people stigmatized by prejudice. Anyone who attended college or graduate school in the last twenty years might think, "Well, what about the women students?" Perhaps because the campaign for women's rights was barely underway during the 1960s, women students either were uninfluenced by the fledging movement or afraid to speak up in class lest they face confused or dismissing reactions from of their mostly older male professors during class or their male classmates outside the classroom. Insensitive comments about women were commonplace and were very rarely challenged by anyone. Both male professors and graduate students felt that women students were fair game for sexual advances. Indeed, there were rumors of sexual contact between male and female students, almost all of whom were married to non-students, and between male professors and female students, whether of not either were married.

Although bigoted comments targeting people of color were rare in class, derogatory remarks about blacks were sometimes heard outside of class during student discussions. Other groups were rarely targeted. Because I migrated to more tolerant people I avoided most of these displays of prejudice. However, a few fellow graduate students with whom I had significant contact were more than willing to use racial epithets. Through interactions with a certain fellow student, I learned that exposure to information which should disconfirm stereotypes, and otherwise discredit prejudice, can have little effect on people who are extreme in their hostility toward people different from themselves. I studied for the prejudice portion of the comprehensive exam with this individual. He could recite all the evidence that profoundly contradicts stereotypes and negative feelings about historically oppressed groups. Yet, as we were studying for the exam, he would freely use racial slurs. One would think that his biases would make it difficult for him to learn the material. Not so. We did equally well on the exam and both passed.

Paula and I selected a duplex garage apartment for our first home. The people on the other side of the thin wall were volatile newlyweds from Mississippi. In public they always seemed to be laughing and smooching. However, we also learned more than we wanted to know about their private life. Through the sparse walls, periodically we could hear all hell break loose. Dishes crashing to the floor, furniture tumbling over, pictures falling off the walls, and the screeching of many familiar and some novel expletives assailed our ears at well above 100 decibels. After several minutes of full-blown war an abrupt cessation of hostilities was accompanied by stone silence. Shortly thereafter we would hear the unmistakable sounds of sexual ecstasy. There was some very well honed method in their madness.

Bobby and Sally, as I'll call them, were congenial if somewhat garrulous people. Sally was usually pleasant, something of the sweet Southern girl, but after the battle behind the apartment wall was replayed several times, we knew she had a temper. Bobby laughed after every other sentence. He seemed to laugh at everything. One day he guffawed uproariously about "taking a hammer to" his brother who had committed a minor offense against him. Thereafter I was more cautious around him. He seemed to be rather impulsive and had some characteristics of a sensation seeker, an impression based on repeated stories about driving fast in the several cars he had owned. He also had the attitudes towards black folks that one would expect of a young, white man who had moved to Houston from Mississippi during the early 1960s.

As proximity is the first rule of social relations, we regularly hung out with Bobby and Sally. Sometimes it was "girls night out" and sometimes "boys night." On one of the latter occasions, Bobby said he was going to take me on a tour of "the best bars" in Houston. That sounded terrific, but I became apprehensive when he revealed what bars he intended to visit. We were going to "n.... town" to experience the black bars.

I became more uptight when he strutted into the first black bar with me creeping along behind him in a submissive posture. Laughing, it seemed to me, even more loudly than usual, he mounted a stool at the bar and ordered us a couple of beers. To my amazement, the all-black bartenders and clientele were utterly insouciant in the face of what I saw as outrageously bold and offensive behavior (there were a few white people in some of the bars we visited later in the evening, mostly women). It took only a few more bar invasions to convince me that white people patronizing black bars was a common occurrence. While it was always obvious that the black patrons of the various bars we visited wanted nothing to do with us, the superficial cordiality of bar personnel made their position clear: white people throwing money around was a tolerable annoyance.

There was clarity on other matters as well. First, at that time no sane black person would enter a bar run by and for white people. It was at the height of the civil rights period. The riots in the Watts section of Los Angeles had already happened and the uprisings of 1967 and 1968 were not far in the future. A black person who wandered into a white bar in Houston would have been in danger of serious bodily harm. Second, Bobby seemed to enjoy flaunting his "right" to invade black people's territory with impunity. Both black and white people knew that whites could do and say what they wanted around black people, even when their words and deeds were clearly designed to offend blacks, but black folks not only lacked the same license, they had to be very cautious around whites.

It was probably the mid-1960s when the four of us went to Memphis to watch Old Miss play the U of H in football. To the delight of my mother, not only were we going to stay in Mississippi during the trip, but we were probably going to witness yet another victory of the Rebels over the Cougars (the two teams played many times during the 1950s and 1960s; when the Cougars finally won a game sometime in the 1960s, Old Miss ended the series). The only occasions upon which Mama teased me were when her alma mater defeated my school.

The game was routine. It was relatively close, but the Rebels prevailed once again. That scene was very different from what occurred when the two teams met in Oxford a couple of years earlier, soon after President Johnson took office. While some friends attended, I stayed home and listened to the game on the radio. Houston had only a couple of black players, but they provided many occasions for Rebel fans to boo loudly and in unison. In one instance, a black Cougar punt receiver, returned a kick some 80 yards for a touchdown. The play took several seconds during which the crowd filled the stadium with a chorus of the most thunderous and heartfelt boos I'd ever heard. My friends returned with tales of Rebel fans surrounding them in the stands yelling about how "your President" (Johnson) was ruining their way of life.

The trip to Mississippi, however, was anything but routine. While there, we accompanied Bobby and Sally to a party. It was one of the few times in my life when I felt seriously fearful. There was talk about n.... s doing this or that in violation of local mores. I heard more than one discussion about what the Klan was going to do to set things right. Rumors were freely floating around the room. Among them was the "fact" that white Nuns who came to the South with other civil rights workers were sleeping with black militants. It seemed that it was the end of the Civil War when the South was allegedly inundated with carpetbaggers and scalawags. I could only think about what I would say if I were asked about the issues under discussion. Fortunately, it didn't happen. I apparently looked like any other "good old boy." They must have assumed I agreed with them, and, to my great shame, I didn't have the courage to speak up. Paula was probably subject to the same assumptions. After all, we had come with people from "down home."

When we made it out of Mississippi, I felt that we had escaped with our lives, but I came to that judgment too quickly. Bobby backed his reputation as a speedster by driving his 1965 Mustang in excess of 100 mph while Paula and I prayed silently in the cramped back seat. After much pleading, I was granted a turn at the wheel. I felt we were all much safer with me at the controls driving at a mere 85 mph. But the police officer who stopped me didn't think so. Bobby laughed until he cried as he examined my ticket and never volunteered to share in paying the penalty.

After leaving the apartment, for reasons I'll soon relate, we didn't hear from Sally and Bobby again. But before I leave them, it seems helpful to consider how black folks might have viewed them. During and after the Civil Rights era, more than once I heard some black people say that they would rather discuss matters of race and civil rights with a "red neck bigot" than a "flaming white liberal." Whites folks, liberals and conservatives alike, harbor biases against people of color. Recent psychological research shows that most white people, even those who regard themselves as untainted by bigotry, display signs of non-conscious bias when their responses are assessed by devices that disclose subtle forms of prejudice. These signs of subtle prejudice—for example a cold tone of voice—displayed by people who are unaware of their biases can be very frustrating to blacks and other targets of prejudice. Little wonder that some black people would rather be faced with a "red neck" who is unafraid to reveal his or her biases than a "white liberal" who seems hypocritical in not acknowledging biases. Perhaps we should be most concerned about white people who turn their unacknowledged biases into behaviors that are detrimental or even dangerous to people of color. In any case, with considerable justification, so-called "red necks" think of themselves as hard working Americans who are in danger of losing their place in our society.

By the way, why do some white people remain blissfully unaware of their prejudices? As I indicated in the discussion of the trip to New York City, some white people deny their own racism so they can make the most if it and remain unaccountable. However, many white people have senses of self that are in large part based on beliefs in justice and fair-mindedness. It shouldn't be surprising that they work hard at avoiding displays of bias, because they would find their own discriminatory words and deeds especially offensive. Some of them succeed in this endeavor and display little or no overt or even subtle racial bias. They tend to be people who have parents that they regard as unprejudiced and who have had close and positive contact with people of color as they were growing up.

By the way, subtle racial bias, assessed with sophisticated electronic and neurological techniques, is being heavily researched in the 2000s. Most whites show racial bias when these techniques are used, even some who are well-intentioned and appear to themselves and others as non-prejudiced. Because Dick Parsons, the black CEO of Time Warner, has recently hired Harvard psychologist Mahzarin Banaji, an expert on use of these techniques, expect to learn more about subtle, non-conscious bias on CNN.

Our apartment was in a pretty good part of town (read that as "a safe white neighborhood"). I happened to witness the aftermath of the only serious crime we knew about during our time in the apartment. After buying some groceries from a convenience store around the corner from our apartment, as I made my way to our car, I heard some groaning and sobbing sounds coming from behind the store. I investigated and found a young woman nude from the waist down lying on the concrete. Her posture and the sounds coming from her made me think of mortally wounded rabbits shot on hunting trips when I was a teenager. I placed my sweater over her and ran back to the store where I asked the clerk to call an ambulance. When they took her to the hospital she was no longer moving or making any sounds. I couldn't sleep for several nights after the horrific incident. During the day, the scene would periodically take over my consciousness. Finally I mustered the courage to return to the store and inquire about the young woman. The clerk said something like, "Oh, she's fine ... fully recovered. It was just a lover's quarrel. Her boyfriend beat her up because she wouldn't have sex." He said it as if the women had violated her boyfriend's rights, and he justifiably took "corrective" action.

Our time in the duplex came to an abrupt end the day Paula violated the "no pets" clause in our contract by bringing home a newborn puppy someone had left in her mother's car. She could not bear to part with it so we attempted to hide it from our landlord. It didn't take him long to discover the dog as he regularly entered our apartment when we were gone without telling us. One day we returned home to find him waiting for us. He told us we would have to move before the end of the month.

Our landlord was an interesting character. Being Greek was the center of his universe. He claimed to know every Greek in Houston, a assertion that seemed outrageous until I reflected on my continuing experience of working in a men's clothing store. Whenever I sold something to a customer whose name was obviously Greek, I asked him whether he knew my fraternity Big Brother, who is Greek. Unfailingly the customer would know my Big Brother and his entire family. Eventually I discovered that "clannishness" among Greeks didn't explain the observation that Houston's Greeks seemed to know each other. Rather, every Greek knowing every other Greek in town is best explained by the fact that, at the time, there was only one Greek Orthodox Church in Houston.

As the end of the month approached, we hastily located a relatively new house with a VA loan that we could assume. It had a brick façade around the lower part of the front with cedar boarding extending from the brick to the roof, a carport, and a chain link fence in the back yard that would accommodate the dog. This stylish little home had three bedrooms, one bath, a modern kitchen and beautiful wooden floors, all for an eighty-five dollar monthly payment. Why such a good deal? It was, if not the first integrated neighborhood in Houston, surely one of the first. Not caring about the ethnicity of our neighbors, we signed on the dotted line.

A Jewish couple lived on one side of us. The house on the other side was used as a church by black neighbors. The neighborhood appeared to have an equal number of black and white homeowners, but on our block and the two surrounding us there were more blacks than whites.

Since most residents were new to the neighborhood, we were surprised at the community spirit that characterized them. Streets and yards were spotless and a neighborhood committee was working on restoring the shuttered community-center building. In addition, there was a movement afoot to eliminate the church. Again, we basically didn't care. The joyous gospel music that awakened us on Sunday morning was magnificent, but there was a reason for some mixed feelings on our part: we tended to party with other graduate-student couples on Saturday night, sometimes until two or three AM. Being awakened at 9:00 AM every Sunday morning was usually not to our liking. Thus, when a black neighbor asked to speak with us about the Church we were happy to listen. Over dinner at our house, we were told that he graduated from Texas Southern University where he played football. Bobby Barlow was smart, articulate, and a well-informed natural-born-leader. More than anyone else, he was responsible for strict community standards and for the rejuvenation of the community center. He felt that the neighborhood was for homes, not churches or businesses. We agreed, as did most of the other residents. The church moved.

There was another aspect of community spirit that was apparently imported from wherever our black neighbors hailed. If something was broken, everybody contributed to fixing it. One day while chatting with a black neighbor I incidentally remarked that my little sports car was not running right. A short time thereafter he had rounded up several neighbors who arrived at our house bearing automotive expertise and tools. After a couple of hours of joking around, drinking some beer and tinkering with my car, it was humming like the day I bought it. Never before or since did we experience this autonomic response to neighbors in need.

But all wasn't hunky-dory. About a year after we moved to the neighborhood, our dog Zany—a play on our former landlord's name and a description of the dog's deportment during puppy-hood—had taken on a formidable wolf-like appearance. One day he escaped our fence and chased a black kid on a bicycle. Apparently the boy panicked, fell off his bike and cut himself on shards of glass from the shattered Coke bottle he was holding. I tried to help, but he made his own way home. As soon as I could I found out where he lived, I dropped by his house, and rang the doorbell in the hope of apologizing and providing compensation for any medical expenses. The boy's father responded to the ring and heard only that I was the offending dog's owner before he slammed the door in my face. I was never able to talk with him further about the incident.

A few days later a white Houston police officer arrived at my house to investigate the dog attack. He sneeringly informed me that he was sorry to bother me, but he was forced to interview me about a complaint by the boy's father. He recorded a few token notes and left after assuring me that nothing would come of the offense ... and nothing did. Partly because of this incident, I have always found black folks' complaints about police brutality and insensitivity to be highly credible.

One day Mama finally arrived on our doorstep. I don't recall whether Daddy was with her—by the time of the visit he was even more the taciturn background figure than he had been in his younger years—but Polly was conspicuously absent. When I asked, "Where's Polly?" Mama hemmed and hawed but finally revealed that Polly didn't know that we lived in an integrated neighborhood. Had she been told, Mama feared she would faint dead away or maybe have a heart attack. Polly was forever spared the alarming news about our neighborhood.

Sometime before I finally completed my graduate studies and we left our vibrant neighborhood for the farm country of Illinois, Polly and I had our last confrontation about race. We had been watching some variety show on TV—Ed Sullivan's show, I think—when Louis Armstrong was introduced, famous trumpet in hand. Polly wasted no time escaping the room. I pursued her to her bedroom door calling after her about how irrational she was acting. She responded that "Negroes" should not be allowed on TV. Further rants on my part only garnered a conversation-ending final retort. "You just don't understand," she mumbled as she closed the door behind her.

Polly died a couple of years after we left Houston. Before she died, I talked repeatedly with family about her condition, but, despite dire reports, I refused to accept that she was terminally ill. Even a discussion with her physician failed to convince me that she was dying. In a state of denial, I boarded a plane to Houston to see for myself whether my family had given up on her too soon. I went directly to her hospital bed and was devastated to find her unresponsive. She was covered with tubes and could not recognize me, let alone talk to me. I had to give up.

After Polly died, I spent a lot of time thinking about her. She was clearly the most important person in my life. Polly lived for her grandchildren, her daughter, and her job. She would do anything for my sisters and I. For example, she recognized the importance of a boy having a nice car to drive. When she needed a new car, I was allowed to select it. In one case, I chose a beautiful bronze 1958 Chevy Biscayne to which I added spinner hubcaps on the front wheels and skirts over the back wheels. When she returned from work at about 5 PM on weekdays she handed the keys to me. Polly also made sure that my sisters had what she thought girls needed: clothes, especially for noteworthy occasions such as formal dances.

When my sisters and I moved away, and she was forced to retire due to her age, she had little left to sustain an interest in living. Years after she was gone my grief took the form of agonizing over the conflict between the affection and admiration I felt for her and the belief that she would be regarded as "racist" by many of the people I came to know during adulthood. At some point I repressed those mixed emotions. Only in recent years have I been able to come to terms with my feelings about her. She was a product of her times. That is not to excuse her beliefs and feelings about race, but it is to acknowledge that even basically decent people can be seduced by the cultural imperatives of their communities. While millions of Americans from both the North and the South once approved of slavery—which is the legacy that sustains our problem with race today—only some of them were truly mean-spirited. The relatively small number of white Americans who opposed slavery—the abolitionists—did so at great risks to themselves and their families. Sadly, too few of us humans, even those with strong character and many fine qualities, have the courage and wisdom to oppose evil when it becomes woven into the fabric of their otherwise humane cultures. Take the case of the world's one billion Muslims. Obviously the vast majority of Muslims are neither radical nor bent on the destruction of non-Muslims. Fortunately, radical Muslims who vow to destroy all who do not accept their view of Islam are a tiny minority of a huge group, though they pose a serious danger. So far, the great majority of Muslims have acted as did many humane whites during the period of slavery in the USA: they have not had the courage or will to rein in radical Muslims, who are resorting to terrorist acts and, thereby, defaming their religious order as they murder thousands of innocents.

Paula's parents were also "products of their time," but their beliefs and feelings about race were more straightforward than those of my parents. Both routinely used the "n" word and saw nothing wrong with it. When Paula, I, and our children admonished them when they used the word, they seemed puzzled. Both were reared in southern Missouri where the use of the word and the open endorsement of stereotypes was an everyday occurrence. Paula's father periodically declared that he had once been a "card carrying member of the Ku Klux Klan," though Paula's mother scoffed at this claim while pointing out that it was most often made when he was in an inebriated state. Yet they lacked the mean-spiritedness one attributed to racists. For example, once they were considering membership in a church. In the course of learning about the church, they were informed that blacks were not allowed to attend services, much less join. Once they learned about the rejection of blacks, they declined to discuss membership further. Unlike my parents, neither did they act like plantation owners in their treatment of the occasional black maid who worked at their house. Maids were treated like everyone else who entered their house: with respect.

One of these maids was a teacher who found willing students in Paula, her mother and I. Mary was an intelligent and attractive woman in her late thirties. She did such an efficient job of cleaning my mother-in-law's house that there was plenty of time to talk with whoever was around. She chatted amiably with my in-laws, but mostly she discussed various issues with Paula and I, as her parents worked all day everyday. During one such conversation, out of the blue Mary asked, "I guess you are wondering why I drive such a high-class car?" in reference to her late model Buick. The car had been discussed around the dinner table. How could a maid afford such an expensive automobile? It was newer and more prestigious than other cars typically seen on the block, including in my in-laws' driveway. Mary answered her own question. "It's what I spend most of my money on—more than the place where I stay—because it gets me some respect. Before I had it people were honking at me in my old wreck and shouting for me to 'get the hell out of the way,' followed by some four-letter words. Now I can drive just about anywhere without people bothering me and sometimes they even get out of my way [it was clear that 'they' meant white people]. I work more jobs than I'd have to if I weren't paying for the car, but it's worth it."

Today, black people and women still must go the extra yard to get respect. Black professional men appear more likely to wear a suit and a tie, even though few of their white-male colleagues dress up. To be taken seriously, professional women appear more likely, in many settings, to dress formerly in non-revealing black and navy blue.

My career as a graduate student was winding down. By the spring of 1968 I had passed my comprehensive exams and gotten approval for my dissertation. A couple of fellow graduate students and I were studying methods to persuade adolescents to take better care of their teeth. Accordingly, we acquired permission to administer experimental procedures to junior high students at their schools. All was going well until April 4, 1968, the day Martin Luther King was assassinated, allegedly, by James Earl Ray. When it was announced that there would be a holiday the following Monday to commemorate Dr. King's life, some of the all-white faculty went ballistic. The ostensible source of these outbursts was adding an additional day to the school year, which meant one day of summer vacation lost. Some members of the all-white faculty were openly cursing King in the hallways, complete with use of the "n" word. We were not surprised as we had earlier been accosted by a faculty member because "your university" invited "that n...." comedian Dick Gregory to speak (I attended his talk and found his iconoclastic and hilarious style to be fascinating). It was as if we had somehow been responsible for Gregory's invitation. We basically didn't respond to these tirades partly because we felt like we were surrounded in hostile territory. But the major reason for our failure to denounce this outrageously bigoted behavior was the fear that we would not only be unable to complete our data collection, we might lose what we had already collected. I can see now that our frightfulness was irrational, but it was based on a vicarious and close-to-home experience: a Latino dissertation student, who graduated before we did, had collected his data in Mexico, but, before he could return to the USA, he was accused of being a CIA spy and the data was confiscated. He had to start all over. Alternatively, perhaps we just didn't have the intestinal fortitude to confront faculty who were spewing racial hatred.

Of course, some white public school personnel reacted quite differently to Dr. King's death. Paula had completed her degree in elementary education and had taken a teaching job at what had to be one of the first black-white integrated elementary schools in Houston (integration started in the early grades). Her elderly white principal was somewhat harsh and very exacting, but, fortunately, liked Paula. Despite her forbidding disposition, she was a fair-minded and humanitarian person who wept openly when she learned of Dr. King's death.

In the spring of 1968, I went on a job hunt at a psychology convention in Chicago and met Dr. James Joyce, chair and founder of the psychology department at Western Illinois University (WIU). He invited me to present my dissertation data to the WIU psychology faculty that summer. It went well and I was hired.

Paula and I were reluctant to leave Houston. For one thing, our families were there. Also, familiarity breeds affection: we had become used to the big city and all its perks. But the position was the best prospect I had, and I really liked the WIU faculty I met. That I tried to sugarcoat my description of WIU's home and the surrounding area—"oceans of gorgeous, green corn and soy bean plants" or something equally disingenuous—would come home to haunt me when Paula actually saw the place.

6

Living in the Great Mid-West

A lot of life change in a short period of time is not good. In fact, it's stressful, even if it involves joyful changes such as getting married or having a baby. We underwent some pretty profound changes when we moved from Houston to Macomb, IL, home of WIU. Obviously, we were going from a sprawling metropolis—well over a million people and covering more area than almost all US cities—to a town of less than 10,000, not counting the 9,000 or so students. There were few restaurants and most of those available were of poor quality. A burger joint and a Dairy Queen were other alternatives for eating out. The nearest mall was in Peoria, a two-hour drive. Local department stores included Montgomery Wards and J. C. Penny's, but both outlets were small and offered very limited varieties of merchandise. There were so few doctors in town that one could expect to spend half a day waiting in line to consult with one. The local hospital was relatively new, but, unlike its status today, it was not up to the standards of that time. The seriously ill had to travel to Peoria, Springfield, or Iowa City. Entertainment was limited to a drive-in and two movie theaters where the latest movies were rarely shown. However, the entertainment and the guest speaker programs at WIU were as good then as they are today—very good. Many famous people visited WIU, including Richard Nixon, Bill Cosby, and Bob Hope. The latter launched his mock US presidential run during a homecoming parade and taped his part in the parade for the Bob Hope television show. Macomb was not an exciting place, but we came to appreciate the warmth of the people and the fact that it was a great place to rear children.

Not only were we settling in a very different place, we were also leaving the people we held most dear. Paula was particularly concerned about leaving her mother. We also were abandoning family members, close friends among graduate, undergraduate, and especially high school classmates, and the lives we loved: the graduate student life and teaching school children. On top of all that, Paula was several months pregnant with our first child. Compared to any other age group, multiple life changes are most likely to afflict young adults and either makes them strong or brings them down.

After a couple of weeks in a motel room, our furniture finally arrived and we moved into a small mouse-infested house with two tiny bedrooms, a cramped kitchen, and what amounted to a hallway that served as a dinning room/living room. While I began to know my colleagues, for a period of several months, Paula had no one but me.

That first semester was kind of a blur for me. Mainly all I can remember about my professional life is the trauma of going back to Houston where I successfully defended my dissertation, which raised my $12,000 salary another $600. It sounded like a lot, but we actually did less well than when Paula was teaching, and I got money as a graduate research assistant under a social psychology grant. No tax obligation in Houston was part of the difference; medical and other preparations for the new baby made up the rest. Though not so weighty as the other sources of change, there was another noteworthy difference: I had taught as a graduate student at the University of Houston, but I encountered my first non-white students at WIU. They were few and far between, but at least there was some diversity.

At the University of Houston, I got approval to do a dissertation in visual perception from a professor who could offer no financial support. When my social psychology professor, under whose grant I received money, learned of my dissertation plans with the visual perception professor, he issued an ultimatum: abandon the perception dissertation or lose my financial support. Being more enamored with food and shelter than autonomy in choosing my research topic, I acquiesced. On the new job I was free from the shackles of graduate-student status, so I could pursue any research topics that interested me. I chose racial bias.

Early in my second semester, our first daughter was born. We gave her our mothers' name, Margaret. Although Paula did most of the parenting and household duties, life got still more complicated for me. Largely through neglecting my classes, thereby alienating my students and facing their anxiety-provoking wrath, I managed to make time to begin my research program. My first act in the research arena was to apply for a grant from the National Institute of Mental Health (NIMH). Probably because my topic was hot at the time, in short order I was granted a substantial sum of money.

Getting a Federal grant at that time was apparently something new at WIU. Shortly after the money arrived I was summoned to an interview with the university publicist. He seemed like a nice guy and appeared to be interested in what I was going to do. I told him that I would recruit WIU students to participate in an experiment in which they would make personal decisions about public figures who were familiar to most people at the time (for example basketball great Wilt Chamberlain and singer Barbara Streisand). When they were asked whether they would enter into an intimate relationship with these well-known black and white people (for example, kin through marriage), I expected that the great majority of white students would more willingly embrace white than black public figures, even the ones who had scored low on a prejudice test. However, I also expected that when they were asked whether they most admired white or black public figures, only low prejudiced students would favor black more than white public figures on the non-intimate admiration measure. Finally, when the admiration experiment was repeated, but this time students were led to believe that they were hooked up to a super lie detector, the white student sample would favor whites over blacks, even the low prejudiced students.

As I was proceeding with the description of my research the publicist became increasingly alarmed as evidenced by a blood-drained face and an expression that bordered on terror. As I was finishing, he mumbled something, folded his notebook, stood up and left. University publications contained nothing about the research until years later.

Nevertheless, the money was accepted and the research was completed. Results were closely in line with the expectations I communicated to the publicist. Of course, the research was a big deal to me, even if it was passé locally. I hoped to hear from some of the various institutions that are part and parcel of our society and are engaged in enterprises for which race is an important consideration. To my great disappointment, only one such institution contacted me about the research. I was excited that the U.S Army was very interested in the research and wanted full information about it. They were provided with all they requested, but I waited in vain for feedback from them.

In the same time frame, I published an article in which I argued that assimilation—the demand that non-white people abandon their minority cultures and adopt the majority culture of their society—was a counter-productive solution to racism. Because it was one of the first articles published solely under my own name, I was proud of it and wanted to show it off. My father was among the few people I asked to look at it. When I queried him about it, his only response was "Well, I guess I'm a racist." Subjects relating to race never came up again.

I must admit that this incident decreased my already flagging admiration for him. Mostly I felt sorry for him. Much was expected of my father when he was a young man, but after some early successes, he experienced little but disappointment. During what I saw as his humiliating tenure as assistant director of a Sears complaint department, he did try to start his own business. Among the products he acquired for sale was a fan with compartments on the side into which frozen packets were placed. It was a cheap air conditioner and it actually worked for a small area. Another was an early digital advertisement shown in a window of a display box. A continuous rubber belt with an ad spelled out by holes punched into it was suspended across two rods implanted into electric motors contained in the box. Green lights in the middle of the apparatus illuminated the belt from its insides so that the ad's message was clearly seen when it passed by the window. Several retailers were interested in these and other products that Daddy had ordered from abroad. His choices of products were almost as creative as his several inventions: a device for retrieving drill bits from wells, a refrigeration device cobbled together in the early part of the last century from scraps of metal and wire, and the previously mentioned fan thermostat fashioned from tin-can tops.

Like most of what happened to Daddy late in his life, these business ventures ended badly. A business partner stole the money Daddy had provided to purchase the merchandise promised to several retailers. The business failed and Daddy became despondent. Before the end of the 1960s a neurologist had declared that he had "hardening of the arteries" which produced senility (today it would be called Alzheimer's disease or dementia due to other sources of brain deterioration). At the time that he was confined to a hospital, he seemed almost comatose.

I recall questioning Daddy's diagnosis during a session with his psychiatrist, a shriveled up, supercilious ghost of a man hiding in the shadows of his office. He treated my questioning of Daddy's diagnosis with contempt and I imagined that it was because he knew that I was a psychology graduate student.

In what seemed like a matter of only a few months, Daddy proved both the neurologist and the psychiatrist wrong. He got steadily better and was released to a nursing home in Austin, Texas. Soon he was fixing every broken electrical or mechanical device in the home. Discussions with the staff made me think he was helping them run the place. After an even shorter stay than at the hospital, he left the home for a private apartment and enrolled in a college accounting program. When he graduated, the church he was attending hired him as their accountant, a position he held for several years. I think that it may have been the happiest time of his life. Not only had he accomplished a miraculous recover in an amazingly short period of time, he was enjoying life in ways that had never occurred to him before. Indices of his change to a new and happier self included that the church staff and minister described him as delight to be around and that he had gotten tipsy drinking beer at a church picnic. He had been a lifetime teetotaler!

Just as he was pleased with himself, my family and I were extremely proud of him. In my mind, the great acclaim he won in college and the success he had as a young professional paled by comparison to his amazing comeback. I learned that children almost always find reasons to love and admire their parents, even if the former come to acknowledge serious shortcomings in the latter.

Although my mother never flew so high or fell so far, reflecting on her life opened my eyes to virtues that I had too long ignored. When I was a teenager, had someone asked me whether my mother was a good cook, I probably would have damned her culinary skills with faint praise. She lived through the depression and the food shortages during World War II. As a result she tended to prepare rather bland meals from whatever was available. We would occasionally have a roast on Sunday, along with potatoes and a vegetable; then we'd eat it for the rest of the week. Mama would save every piece of uneaten meat, and scraps of whatever went with the roast, sometimes scraping the meat bone until it looked like it had been bleached in the sun. The concoction we had later in the week was called "hash" and was composed of re-cooked or warmed up bits and pieces left over from previous meals. My appetite often disappeared when I heard the word "hash." Oh, and sometimes the meat was actually cow tongue.

After we moved to Macomb and returned to visit family in Houston, it was a very different story. The hash cook became the gourmet chef. We had spreads of fruit, shrimp, elaborate salads, and several entrees with French names. It was marvelous. I used to compete with my brother-in-law for the best "stuff." It was extraordinary that I never knew Mama was a great cook until I was in my late twenties.

Sadly, it was upon reflecting back to when I was living at home while an undergraduate that I recognized she was a wonderful, caring teacher. She tutored children and adult dropouts at our house. One of the latter was a man in his late thirties or early forties, who had never learned to read. He was a phone company employee who would have failed to pass the test for a desired promotion but, in the act of attempting the test, also would have revealed his deficiency.

I'll never forget Mama's infinite patience and soft encouragement as she brought him from embarrassingly halting attempts at children's books—"TaTa Tommy thra thra thru tha ba ba ball."—to mastering whatever he wanted to read. He got his promotion and repeatedly told

Mama that he could never have done it without her. As he moved up the ladder, he informed her of each advance in his career and she basked in his reflected glory. That she was thrilled with her role in this man's successes fits well with psychological research that shows people who help others benefit even more than the recipients of their altruistic acts. I don't know how well I've done, but during my forty years of teaching I've tried to live up to Mama's high standards.

7

Parenting, "Getting" the Women's Movement, and Relations with Black Folks

This chapter's title may bring to mind an issue that may be written between the lines of earlier chapters. If this book is about race (and it is), why mix in considerations of women's rights and oppression of ethnic groups such as Latinos, Jews and American Indians? First, elsewhere I've written about the lack of scientific evidence for "races." In view of the suspect status of "races" it may be better to collapse "racial" and "ethnic" groups into one category having a label such as "cultural groups" or one with a similar meaning. Second, the various "isms" are all closely related. Thus, women historically have been and continue to be limited and subjugated in ways that resemble the treatment of "racial" groups. Individuals who show bias against blacks are likely to discriminate against women, gay/lesbian people, and people with disabilities. If there is to be a better understanding of the obsession with "race" in the USA we must consider a larger picture. Racial prejudice does not operate in isolation from other forms of bigotry.

Margaret was born in 1969 and Kathleen in 1972. Now Paula had two small children to take care of. I put it that way, because I was contributing little in terms of childcare. Margaret was very attached to her mother. Even though I felt left out, it never occurred to me that Margaret and I might have been closer had I spent more time with her. But I didn't have a clue. I assumed that childrearing was for women—after all my father never helped with my sisters and I. Further, at a time when I was becoming known locally as a defender of civil rights I had no understanding of the women's movement.

In 1973, scarcely one year after Kathleen was born, we had a third child, Bem III (he was actually the sixth across both the Allen and the Price families). Pretty quickly, it became obvious to me that taking care of three children, including two babies, was too much for anyone. So, to a significant degree, I took over parenting Kathleen, while Paula parented Margaret and baby Bem. In reflecting on this change in me, I am reminded of some research about our primate cousins, baboons. In the absence of adult female baboons, male baboons housed with infants not only take over parenting chores but do a pretty good job of it. Perhaps I was like those baboons. I got into parenting by default. In any case, male primates appear to be fully capable of caring for their offspring, they just don't do it except in emergencies.

When Bem was still a baby, Paula and I were invited to a picnic. We were told in advance that there would be "underprivileged children" there, but the significance of that "heads up" was not clear. Indeed, several black children from East St. Louis, Illinois were present. One of them stuck out. She was stocky kid whose hands were constantly formed into fists and whose blank expression changed to a very angry glare as soon as anyone looked at her. This girl was ready to fight.

As the afternoon wore on, one of the picnic's sponsors approached us and asked if we would be willing to invite a child from East St. Louis into our home for a few days. The goal was to give these kids an idea of what rural life was like. In retrospect, I see myself as looking and sounding like Homer Simpson when I agreed to bring an East St. Louis child to Macomb: "Duh, ok." Though I don't remember my actual response, there may have been something in it that cued the person making the request to ask, "You don't have any objections to having black kids in your home, do you?" I assured him that I did not.

So we agreed to pick up two East St. Louis elementary school aged girls, Eugenia and Cynthia Parker, and bring them to Macomb for a stay at our house. A couple of weeks later, when we pulled up in front of their house, out came the two girls, their mother, Mary, and three other kids, a boy named Adrian and two little girls, Latitia, and Leslie. All of latter three were begging to come along, but the little boy was also sobbing loudly. He felt that he was big enough to leave his Mom and couldn't understand why he was being left behind. After some discussion, Mary granted Adrian permission to accompany us. We answered Mary's questions about how she could contact us and when we would bring the children back. Then we assured her that the kids would be well cared for. Finally, we left after promising the little girls that they could come visit us when they were older.

On the way home we stopped by a fast-food restaurant for lunch simply because it was lunchtime. To our amazement, eating out at a hamburger joint was an auspicious occasion for these kids. It had been a long time since they had visited one of these restaurants, but the "delicious" hamburgers, tasty fries, and yummy desserts were children's lore in their neighborhood. So they ordered what they wanted and all eat voraciously, except for Adrian. Adrian's face was formed into a marvelous smile; he was having his hamburger instead of eating it, which he had no inclination to do. Instead he played with a tiny umbrella that came with his meal. Because I was a part of the "eat everything on your plate" white-middle-class generation (and had never experienced an empty plate), I began to badger Adrian about "eating your food," just as my mother had done to me when I failed to finish my meal. Several minutes of this insensitive behavior erased Adrian's joyful grin and replaced it with a rueful look. More minutes must have gone by before I noticed that a middle-aged black woman seated nearby was scowling at me as I scolded Adrian. I ceased my tirade and sat back puzzled. What's the big deal with trying to get a kid to eat his food? However, on the way home I came up with some dire interpretations of my behavior toward Adrian. Although I argued to myself that there was nothing wrong with my traditions and values, I admitted that I had no right forcing them on someone else's child. Basically I was assuming that he had the full range of experiences that I enjoyed when I was his age. Further, I was acting as if there was something almost righteous about cleaning one's plate. Had I been conscious of my privileged status, I might have realized that having something one almost never gets is more important than immediately exploiting its narrowly defined benefits.

Despite this incident, the first trip went well. Our guests seemed to enjoy their time in Macomb. They took pleasure in roaming freely throughout the neighborhood and in taking trips to places like the skating rink and the Dairy Queen. However, when it was time to go back to East St. Louis they seemed sad and reluctant to leave. After talking to them and watching their behavior Paula and I formed hypotheses about their reluctance to return to their home. First, we dismissed out of hand the possibility that they didn't want to leave us. There hadn't been enough time for "bonding" in any sense of the word. A much more reasonable hypothesis was in regard to the neighborhood to which they were returning. They told us that there were bullies living nearby and related that they were worried about someone stealing their bicycles and other valued possessions. These complaints might be lodged against conditions in any impoverished community, but were certainly candidates for reasons not to go home. Also, we were able to give them some privileges and goodies that were probably rarely available at home. Their mother could infrequently afford to take them to fast food restaurants or to other desirable places, such as to the movies. We also had plenty of junk food to which they had open access. In addition, we offered them meats, potatoes and vegetables. True, they didn't like all of the "good" foods we served—most especially "round steak" which they heard as "round snake" (they declined to eat that evening)—but they displayed strong if not voracious appetites. While all these hypotheses may have had some merit, it was not difficult to persuade them to return home: they missed their mother, sisters and their friends.

For the next few years, they returned annually or even more frequently. Not all of the same children returned each visit. In time, Cynthia missed some trips due to work and commitments to friends. The same was sometimes true of Eugenia, though she missed few trips. However, Latitia and Leslie visited regularly after they were old enough to leave home and Adrian made every trip until he approached adolescence.

Eugenia seemed particularly intelligent. We thought she could attend a challenging college or university and do very well. She was quick to pick up on what was going on around her and did very well at the several board games we played with the children, some of which involved significant cognitive skills. As to quick wittedness, she often observed and commented on what she saw in Macomb. One summer day as we were driving around our town she sarcastically remarked, "Oh look, a n ..." This caustic observation took me by surprise, but I caught on after a moment. Eugenia, as I learned over time, was given to pithy statements. In this case she had aptly and succinctly summed up the state of cultural diversity in Macomb: almost everybody was white. While the black student population at the university was big enough to be noticed by the mid-1970s, the town itself had very few black families.

Was this condition at least partly due to discrimination? Of course it was. One would be hard pressed to find a long established town in the USA of any appreciable size that didn't have at least some history of discrimination. Although Macomb was a stop on the Civil War era "underground railroad," which ferried escaped slaves from the South to the North, it has its own history of racial discrimination. For example, Dr. C. T. Vivian, a friend and colleague of Dr. Martin Luther King, and a notable civil-rights worker in his own right, grew up in Macomb and went to WIU. He recalls repeatedly being subjected to the "n" word and to other humiliations during his years here (today there is a street on campus named after him). Until sometime in the 1980s it was rumored that real estate agents confined blacks to the relatively impoverished East side of town. In fact, finding them elsewhere during the 1970s was hard to do (a few black WIU employees did find homes in other parts of town).

Also, the Klan was periodically active in the area. During the 1980s, a cross burning occurred in the yard of a black WIU employee. Only a few years ago, two white men claiming to be Klan members were sent to jail for repeatedly harassing a "mixed" couple (one black and one white). During the 1990s Paula and I and some friends protested a Klan rally held about 30 miles from Macomb. While refueling after the rally, we struck up a conversation with a white farmer who also was gassing up. He remarked, "I don't know what they're [the Klan] doing here. We ain't got no 'n.... s' round here." A couple of years later the Klan wanted to rally in Macomb, but public sentiment turned them away.

All of these tales being told, Macomb is unusual in that its citizens are uncommonly fair-minded. Today, signs of discrimination are much harder to find. Even in the 1970s, the children from East St. Louis apparently felt comfortable in Macomb, a possibility that is supported by their expressed desire to return many times. In fact, in some ways, they were well received. The Macomb Journal published a very thoughtful article about them, complete with a group photo of the Parker and Allen children as well as Paula and me.

Margaret was the only one of our children who was old enough to remember the early visits of the Parker children. She was mature enough to have friends and be concerned about losing them. Among her recollections was that one of her friends wanted to know why we had "n.... s living with us." This same friend said that her mother would not allow her to visit our house while the "n.... s are there." During visits by the Parker children, Margaret began going to friends' houses rather than inviting them over to our house. When the Parker children returned after son Bem had reached social maturity, he recalled hearing neighborhood kids yelling racial epithets at our guests from outside our house. Not so incidentally, after reading a draft of this book, Bem remarked that these kids were not really "friends," a term that I used earlier instead of "neighborhood kids."

Recently Kathleen related how she had "learned" from someone (she thinks it was a playmate) that white people would turn black if touched by a black person. While playing with Latitia one day, our guest reached out to touch Kathleen. When Kathleen avoided contact, Latitia teasingly persisted until she touched Kathleen. At that point, Kathleen revealed why she had resisted Latitia's touch. The latter's response was some good-natured laughing. That reaction, and the fact that Kathleen didn't turn black, was enough to discredit the absurd belief. Paula and I were blissfully unaware of these incidents and only recently learned about them.

Years after the Parker children reached adulthood, they continued to communicate with us. In periodic phone calls from one or another of them, they seemed optimistic. Eugenia and Latitia were planning for an advanced education and both eventually attended local colleges for a time. Adrian was studying to be a chef and Cynthia was married and had a child. Leslie, the youngest, had not revealed her future plans.

Mary's lot was not so sanguine. In the early years, when we traveled to East St. Louis to pick up the kids, she was bubbling-over-happy with her job as a teacher's aide. She really felt that she was making a contribution. Eventually, though, she lost the job due to government cuts in educational funding. Thereafter, her children reported that she was lethargic and sad. When we talked to her she complained of many ailments. It seemed to me that she was seriously depressed. Little wonder. Mary's opportunity to make worthwhile contributions to the school children she served, and to bolster her own wellbeing in the process, was suddenly and capriciously taken away. Hers was a classic case of an individual who generously helped others and, in so doing, benefited at least as much as those she served. When government proposes eliminating services, it should consider those who will be deprived of serving as much as those who are served. I believe that Mary's early demise, well before she had the opportunity to meet most of her grandchildren, can, at least in part, be laid at the door of disappointment.

Eugenia died of a ruptured aneurysm in her mid-thirties. Under more favorable life circumstances her medical problem would likely have been diagnosed in time, and she would have achieved a great deal of success in life. She was a smart, decent, and attractive person. Sadly not all of those with her fine qualities realize the American Dream.

The last time we heard from Latitia, she was in the armed forces and planning to continue her college education after completing her military obligation. She described Adrian as something of a traveling man, moving his large family around as he took jobs ranging from cook to circus worker. We hope to hear good news about the Parkers in the years to come.

By the early 1970s I was fully identified as the "white guy who knew about black people." This obviously absurd perception on the part of others was difficult to combat. At first I tried to defeat this misconception and its ridiculous implications by informing white colleagues that "black people" denotes a very large group of individuals who differ greatly along each of many, many dimensions, such that no one could speak for all of them, much less a white person. Finally, I gave up and resorted to sarcasm. For example, because some white colleagues hinted that I must really be black or else I wouldn't be advocating for black people (no kidding), I suggested that, indeed, my family was black. At a 1970s party for a colleague who was moving on to another job, we all "roasted" the departing friend, each other, and ourselves. When it was my turn, I suggested that if all present took a closer look at the Allen children, they would see that our kids got more than a little dark after brief exposure to the summer sun. There was no laughter, no smirking—wannabes were as yet unheard of—just silence. I imagined that they took me seriously.

Not surprisingly, as there were no black professors in my department, like it or not, I became the go-to guy when questions regarding "black issues" arose. In one such case, a white, male student and his black girl-friend were sent to me for advice. They planned to get married, but both sets of parents opposed the union. During a discussion of about an hour the young man informed me that he was an adoptee and that his parents had promised to disinherit him if he married a black woman. The young woman said that her father was so vehemently opposed to the union that they were hiding from him. Aside from parental disapproval, this was a time in which "mixed" couples were likely to be harassed almost anywhere in the USA they might settle. So we jointly concluded that they would lose their parents' affection, and all that goes with it, as well as face even dangerous discrimination walking the streets of most American cities. Still, they wanted to be married so we considered exceptions to the rule that "mixed" couples are not safe most places. Some large cities, such as New York City and San Francisco, did contain neighborhoods where "mixed" couples lived safely. I wished them well and they left my office looking like two young people much in love.

At the time the "Romeo and Juliet" effect was being investigated in the psychological literature: parental interference in their offspring's romantic relations only makes the couple closer. Because I was familiar with this literature I could not help but wonder whether these two were together at least in part to defy their parents. While such may be true in many cases, whether or not "mixed" races are involved, it seemed to me that, before we talked, the couple already was very familiar with the dangers and difficulties they would face. By the end of our discussion, they seemed even more convinced that they would face very difficult circumstances if they married. Surely consideration of a harsh future would outweigh a covert need to defy parents. I looked forward to learning of their fate, but never heard from them again.

So what about "interracial" marriage? One interesting question regarding it is whether its increase will contribute to ending racism in the USA or will that increase be a sign that racism is dying. I choose the latter, although to this day, "mixed" marriages are a small, but progressively growing percentage of total marriages. As people come to be less concerned about race there will be less pressure on individuals to avoid falling in love with someone of "another race." This trend toward indifference to race would be consistent with a recognition that, scientifically speaking, there are no "races": there are no groups of people on this earth who are so genetically distinct that they can be called a separate "race." Of the some 50,000 or so human genes, most have effects that are beneath the skin; only a few genes generate the superficial effects which convince too many of us that humans can be separated into different "racial" groups. Almost all of the rest of the differences we "see" are cultural. To put the lack of "races" in perspective, one of the leading scientists working on one of the two human genome projects made the following observation: two people chosen at random from different parts of the world would share 99.9% of their genes.

I don't recall how and under what circumstances I met Don Poindexter, a black psychology student. Perhaps Don had a question about race and was sent to me by a white colleague who professed to know nothing about the subject, but thought I knew much about it. Or maybe Don had a question about the psychology of prejudice and a black colleague sent him to me, because she or he could think of no one else in psychology to recommend. In any case, we immediately struck up a friendship based on our mutual need to understand the dynamics of race on our campus. Don was an obviously bright, energetic, and articulate young man with all the makings of a leader. Indeed, as I came to know him I found that wherever I mentioned his name on campus someone had heard of him. Later I found out that, not only was he a leader among students, he was also one of a few black students that the administration called upon when there was a danger of "unrest."

During the late 1960s and early 1970s, Don was among only 100 to 150 black students in a WIU student population ranging from 10,000 to over 13,000 (he graduated in 1974). He spoke with anguish about feeling that he was under a microscope most of the time. For example, students actually came to watch him shower to marvel at his prodigious muscula-ture, which provided them with an explanation of his athletic prowess. Many knew that Don had been a high school football and baseball star in Peoria and that he signed a professional baseball contract with the Califor-nia Angels. He made it to the triple-A level before an old football-knee-injury ended his career.

Because he became known as "that smart black guy," students expected that he would be "smart" in every way. In reality, Don was embarrassed that he could not excel in every arena. He once lamented his lack of back-ground in math and described his first math class at WIU as an experience in "cultural shock." [Not so incidentally, research by black psychologist Claude Steele and his colleagues has shown that stereotypes about innu-meracy among blacks and women have become self-fulfilling prophesies: highly gifted blacks and women score lower on a math test than equally gifted whites and men, respectively, only if they are reminded of their alleged deficiency in math before the test; without the reminder, they score the same as their counterparts.] He also worried about his academic stand-ing because he was in such high demand as a spokesperson for black peo-ple that he had limited time to study.

Despite these pressures Don continued to be effective as a commentator on the campus racial scene without claiming to be speaking for all black students. He was the second president of the Black Student Association and a frequent speaker on civil rights both on and off campus. In psychol-ogy, his major, he sought a way to attract black students to the discipline and keep them from fleeing the nearly all-white classes for courses in other disciplines where they would be more likely to encounter people like themselves. To promote a more comfortable atmosphere for black psychology students he proposed that the department start a "Black Student Psychological Association" (BSPA). Because psychology had no black faculty, he turned to me as faculty sponsor of the BSPA. The organization got off to a good start, with each meeting attracting a large portion of the small number of black psychology students. Quite naturally, he was elected to be the first President of the BSPA and presided over meetings.

Among the good ideas that came out of the BSPA were efforts to get black students involved in psychological research. Don provided himself as a model for other black psychology students by launching a research project. He strolled through black neighborhoods in Peoria and Chicago stopping people to recruit them as subjects. Participants were asked to inspect pictures of black men who varied from very dark to very light in skin color in order to test his hypothesis that black people were more likely to believe that light-skinned blacks have higher status occupations than dark skinned-blacks. Results only partially supported his hypothesis. Nevertheless, his creative thinking put him ahead of his times. In recent years there has been an accumulation of experiments that show light-skinned people—regardless of how they are identified by other cues such as hair texture—are favored over dark-skinned people even by black subjects. A recent widely reported survey revealed that, regardless of race, light-skinned people make significantly more money than dark-skinned people. Skin color seems to have a life of its own beyond its connection to race. Both white and black experimental subjects tend to lump together light-skinned people, and separately group together dark-skinned people, such that light-skinned people are seen as highly similar to each other and dark-skinned people are also seen as highly similar to each other.

Internationally, it is difficult to find a place where light-skin is not preferred over dark-skin. For example, in the outstanding movie entitled "Water," which was set in India, the mother of the male protagonist responds to her son's announcement that he has selected a wife with, "Is she light-skinned?" In several South and Central American countries, until recently, almost all heads of state have been of European heritage (Spanish or Portuguese). When a newspaper columnist bought the freedom of a young South East Asian sex slave, he paid a premium price, because she is light-skinned. One obvious explanation of this remarkable phenomenon is the historical, worldwide subjugation of dark-skinned people by light-skinned people.

Sadly, Don's life ended in tragedy. During the 1980s I had heard that he was a successful psychological counselor in Peoria, but learned nothing else about him until his death made front-page news in the Peoria Journal Star (PJS) at the end of 1985 and the beginning of 1986. The PJS revealed that Don was a heroic figure who piled failures on top of successes during a life of often changing professional pursuits. In his early forties, Don died of heart failure during a pickup basketball game. At the time of his death, he was in a prison work-release program after having been convicted of passing bad checks. His best friend at WIU, the founder of Black Student Association and now a successful businessman, reminisced about Don in one of the PJS newspaper articles. His college buddy recalled that Don was multi-talented, a born leader, and a person who would say the right thing at the right time. However, he often contrived ways to use the situations in which he found himself. Related to this perception, I recall a reason why he rarely sustained whatever he was pursuing professionally: Don felt he could never catch a break from "the man" (powerful white men). Thus, life had become a game in which Don felt he had to use underhanded methods to get past the barriers placed in his path. Had his early life experiences with white people been different he would surely have had a different attitude, one that would have made him a continuing success. As it was, Don became yet another black man with great talents who never experienced complete and continuous success, in part because of his experience-based assumption that just when he approached the pinnacle of achievement, he would be held back. In an attempt to lessen the likelihood of such tragic disappointments in the future, a scholarship for students of color was created in Don's name soon after his death.

The BSPA continued for some time after Don graduated and sponsored or co-sponsored some important events. During the mid-1970s it was partly responsible for bringing a very well known and respected black psychologist to WIU. This individual, who I'll call Dr. Wilson, had made and would continue to make news both within and outside of psychology through his insightful and sometimes controversial ideas. Dr. Wilson brought a young black man with him who was just completing his Ph.D. in clinical psychology, but planned to enter medical school rather than use his new degree. He announced that he could do more good in black communities as a physician than as a psychologist. In announcing his abandonment of psychology he created a confrontational atmosphere in which the expression of anger toward the discipline became the order of the day. Indeed, as I have indicated elsewhere, there are legitimate reasons for black psychologists to be upset with psychology. Racist psychologists have infested American psychology's organizations almost from the beginning of the discipline in the USA. One even managed to head the American Psychological Association during the late 1940s and some still are having impact today, though their numbers and influence are waning. The difference between then and now is that damaging assertions—such as claiming that blacks have smaller brains than whites and, thus, are doomed to suffer lower intelligence—were then assumed to be "scientific fact" by too many psychologists, but are now being successfully challenged.

Dr. Wilson had more personal and general reasons for being angry. This obviously brilliant man, whose contributions are likely to be remembered longer than the works of almost all psychologists alive today, had experienced roadblocks erected in his academic and professional path throughout his life. He told the audience during the session with the young physician-to-be that a white high school counselor had told him that he should forget about college and learn to be a laborer. I have never before or since attended a public meeting during which so much anger was expressed with so much justification.

The evening after the contentious session, black faculty from other departments and black students from several departments, including psychology, arranged a party at a black faculty member's house. I was invited and attended. Despite being the only white person in a crowd of some fifty people, I felt comfortable because the students interacted with me throughout the evening. We drank, we talked, we even danced. All the while Dr. Wilson glowered at me. I couldn't blame him. Had I lived his life I probably would have been even angrier.

In this same time frame, Paula and I were asked if we would sponsor an international student. Once again, we said "yes" without thinking about the implications of our commitment. Just as in the case of the "kids from East St. Louis" our thoughtless compliance with someone's request resulted in some fascinating, enlightening, and enjoyable experiences.

It turned out that our "foreign student" was from Nigeria. 'Yinka Vidal (a.k.a. Victor Vidal) was studying medical technology at WIU and, at the same time, trying to find a way to bring his family to the USA. Victor was a bright young man with enormous energy and determination to succeed. Once he set a goal, he would not rest until he reached it. The first hurdle he wanted to jump was learning to drive. My job was to take him out into the country where the roads were relatively deserted so that lessons would be "safe."

At the time we had a car that may have been our best-ever-bargain in modes of transportation. It was 1965 Ford LTD sedan that I had purchased for $100. The faded gold exterior was interrupted every few inches by patches of rust. Apparently the farmer who had owned it used it as a truck and chicken coop. The interior was covered with chicken feces, dirt, mold and some unidentifiable substances. Nails and other pieces of metal, including a steel bar, were fused to the carpeting by accumulations of rust. It took us days to clean this much-abused vehicle, but it was worth it (though our children didn't think so; when they got older, they were embarrassed to ride in it). After clearing away the exterior rust and the interior crud, we had what proved to be a solid and reliable automobile. Driving lessons for Victor provided me with the first of many adventures in our $100 wonder, which our kids affectionately dubbed the "Clunker."

So here we were hurdling down a seriously pitted two-lane country road, Victor grinning excitedly behind the wheel and me in the passenger seat clinging to the dashboard. As we swerved about and bounced dangerously near a yawning ditch I shouted, "slow down" "pull over!" "STOP!" Victor, who was highly proficient in English—the common language of

Nigeria—seemed not to hear me. It appeared that he had a great need for speed. Very soon, the inevitable happened: we ended up in the ditch.

As neither of us were hurt, our attention immediately focused on how we might extricate ourselves from the aftermath of his accident. Fortunately, a farmer was working his fields nearby and immediately stopped what he was doing to find out what the fuss was about. The farmer was a tall, stern man who seemed unsurprised at our predicament. Talking to him after he quickly and efficiently pulled us from the ditch with his tractor, it became clear that he had extracted lots of folks "from the city" out of ditches and fields. So he accepted our many thank-yous and politely declined our offer of remuneration. As I learned over the years, he was typical of farm people. They are self-reliant and hard working family folk, who can always be counted on to help whoever happens by and suffers some mishap. Sadly, as family farms die out, farmers' tradition of relying on themselves and, at the same time, generously offering help to others, is likely to fade into history. If so, a precious part of Americana will be gone forever.

Victor mastered driving in record time. A couple of weeks after the Clunker was hauled from the ditch, he informed me that he had purchased a car and driven to Chicago often attaining speeds in excess of 100 mph. My state of alarm didn't subside until several weeks passed and nothing bad happened.

Victor was in and out of our lives. He came by our house for dinner now again, but between these sporadic visits he was out of touch for long periods of time. To our surprise, after months of no word from him, he showed up at our door wanting a loan to help pay for his family's transportation to the USA. At the time we were as broke as we would ever be, typically running out of money before the end of the month. So, we had no trouble reaching a decision about his request; there was no way we could help him. He thanked us profusely for considering his request, then again disappeared for months. The next time we heard from him he had more surprising news. His wife and children had made it to America and he was headed for graduate school at what is now the University of Illinois at Springfield. There he earned a masters degree in psychology and also received training in pharmacology. After graduation, he and his family returned to Nigeria. There he worked and trained at the Lagos College of Medicine. Later they settled in St. Louis where he worked in and then headed a medical school laboratory. All that we learned about Victor after he told us about entering graduate school at the U of I in Springfield was in his autobiography mailed to us in February of 1994. Because, at the time, I was heavily invested in family as well as research and teaching, I planned to scan the book and lay it aside. But once I got into it, I couldn't put it down. It was a remarkable chronicle of an African Man's struggles to succeed in "American Medicine," a set of rigid traditions that defined no place for him. And succeed he did despite the bad odds.

Victor's life in America provides a good illustration of Nigerian-born University of California Anthropology Professor John Ogbu's theory regarding "voluntary" and "involuntary" black immigrants to the USA. African Americans were "involuntary" immigrants because they were brought here as slaves and were taught throughout their history in the USA that "you can't make it in America." Even today, talented black students are receiving a subtle message that they are expected not to succeed (recall the discussion of Claude Steele's research on self-fulfilling nature of stereotypes about women's and minorities' alleged deficiencies). By contrast, "voluntary" black immigrants from Africa and Haiti come here with no knowledge of the barriers that have stifled African Americans' ambitions. Black immigrants from elsewhere enter America expecting to succeed and often do so despite attempts to fit them with the manacles that have historically shackled African Americans. For example, Haitians in New York City are making enough money to place them near the average income for New Yorkers, which makes them one of the most successful minorities in the city.

By the mid-1970s I felt that I "had a clue" about race and all its implications, but about the Women's Movement and "women's rights" I had none. I must have been asking myself, "What do women want?" Freud, who famously posed the question, died without finding an answer. My feeble searches for an answer left me dumbfounded. But, believe it or not,

I was about to get a clue or two in the process of teaching a course in experimental social psychology.

When I designed the course, I planned many one-on-one sessions with students during which we would talk about their projects. We talked about their initial ideas, about their written proposals and, after I approved of their projects, about the data they collected and about drafts of their final papers. The fact that there were a disproportionate number of women in the class puzzled me until I talked to them at length. They wanted to apply the scientific method to understanding bias against women.

I'll describe just one example of the kinds of topics that women students found interesting and relevant to women's issues. During the 1970s, a line of research compared ratings of the exact same essays attributed to a female author for some experimental subjects and to a male author for other subjects. Results consistently showed that ratings of a given essay were more positive if subjects thought it was authored by a man than if they thought it was authored by a woman. Several women students designed experiments to further examine this variety of sex bias while other women students studied additional issues related to bias against women. As it turned out, by the time these women students were researching the sex-of-author bias, overt bias against women looked as if it was fading. One woman student found no bias against women even when subjects were hooked up to what they thought was a super lie detector that could "read your inner most thoughts." Another woman student did find sex bias against women using a variation of the super lie detector method, without all the fancy equipment. Results were frustratingly mixed.

Many years later psychologists Peter Glick and Susan Fiske showed that men, and sometimes women, are ambivalent about women. People tend to harbor both hostile sexism and benevolent sexism, with the former involving all the negative stereotypes about women (can't do math, too emotional, etc.) and the latter entailing all the positive stereotypes (nurturing, concerned about others' feelings, etc.). [Note that the "positive stereotypes" about women tend to connote low power compared to the many positive stereotypes about men that you can undoubtedly conjure.] The same person can harbor both of these two types of sexism and display one or the other depending on the demands of the situations in which they find themselves. These mixed feelings about women might explain the mixed results found by the women in my research class.

But, because hostile and benevolent sexism were findings of the future, we were, at the time, stuck with confusing results about how women are regarded. During many in-depth discussions, women students and I tried to resolve these inconsistent results about bias against women. Over time I began to "get it" as well as a man can. It began to occur to me that there is an answer to Freud's question, "What do women want?" Susan B. Anthony put it succinctly: "… men, their rights and nothing more; women, their rights and nothing less."

These revelations led to changes in me, some of it relatively trivial—I quit subscribing to Playboy magazine after becoming convinced that its displays of women in the nude painted a monolithic picture of them that could be as dangerous as it was limiting—to the more meaningful—I joined NOW—to actively supporting women's rights—the whole family went to Springfield, IL in 1979 to rally for the Equal Rights Amendment (talking about short and sweet, the ERA simply reads, "Equality of rights under the law shall not be denied or abridged by the United States or by any State on account of sex.") The march on Springfield was fascinating (and transforming) for me and became a turning point for all of us: we got into human rights as a family.

While the clear majority of people present at the 1979 rally for ERA were women, all kinds of people were present. The large crowd included gay people, Latinas, blacks, Asians and one significant contingent of men: dozens of men representing unions were present. The whole experience was a reminder that no one can expect to enjoy inalienable human rights unless everyone does. Deny rights to one group of people and the door is open to denying rights to any number of other groups of people.

Our three children carried their self-constructed pro-ERA signs and reveled in the positive attention they received. Kathleen, who was only seven at the time, remembers the chants: "Thompson remember, we vote in November"; "Equal rights, equal pay, ratify the ERA!" ("Thompson" referred to then Illinois Governor, James R. Thompson). I believe that

Kathleen and Margaret grew up to be feminists, and Bem III fell in love with and married a defender of women's rights, at least in small part because of our day in Springfield.

8

Ethnic Diversity: Getting Started

By the end of the 1970s my research interests had turned to the study of personality. My continued interest in racism and related forms of bias began to be expressed in writings, in teaching, and in on-campus activism. I integrated units on racism and sexism and other forms of bias into courses ranging from introductory psychology to "sensation and perception," all about the human senses. In the early 1980s I wrote the first draft of a novel that was finally published in 2000. Obscurely entitled "World War II: 1939–1948," the book was about changing a few key events that occurred during WWII such that the Nazis won in Europe and successfully invaded the USA. I had hoped to show that had Hitler come to America, his form of racism would have meshed with our own such that many thousands of Americans would have cooperated with him, though many millions would have opposed him. In 1986, friend and colleague Charles Potkay and I published a text on personality that contained coverage of racism and sexism. I also published Personality texts in 1990 and 1994 that followed the same trend. All of these efforts involved talking and writing rather than getting something concrete done. It was talking the talk, but not yet walking the walk.

After years of struggle, in the mid-1980s Marine Magliocco, Janice Welsch, and several other faculty women got the funding needed to open a Women's Center at WIU. Maurine ran the center during many of its early years. The Center became a catalyst for activities by those who sought a broader representation on campus for the various American ethnic groups, especially people of color who, at the time, were rarely found at the head of classrooms or occupying students' chairs. I became acquainted with women leaders on campus when the WIU Administration appointed me to membership on the Center's Board of Directors (during an acute attack of paranoia I thought the Administration wanted me to spy on "women trouble-makers," but there was never any evidence to support my delusions). I was made to feel very comfortable at meetings and soon learned that feminists, in their campaign for women's rights, tend to include all American groups who have historically been denied unfettered pursuit of the American Dream. They also welcomed men who supported human rights. Consistent with these observations, when the time was ripe for adding a little color to a nearly all-white campus, women took the lead.

As I recall, Jan Welsch, a best friend of Paula and I over the years, recommended that I attend a mid-1980s meeting which was to be a forum for considering strategies to increase not only the presence of more people of color on campus, but also to raise students' consciousness about the growing diversity of the American population (already it was evident that someday—now projected to be the middle of the 2000s—non-whites would be the majority of the USA population). I'm not sure exactly who was present at the meeting, but nearly all of those present were women. I believe the group included Jan, Maurine, Polly Radish who would become the head the our Women's Studies Program, Essie Rutledge who at one time headed the National Association of Black Social Workers and was a tireless advocate for equal representation on campus, and Rebecca Parker who seemed always to be present when human rights issues were considered.

I recall that this meeting was the genesis of efforts to recruit more faculty and students of color and to create an atmosphere on campus that would be comfortable for non-white members of the university community. Early efforts were aimed at recruitment of blacks. Unfortunately, it became immediately apparent that any attempts to attract black students and faculty involved a variation of the old chicken and egg problem. Before it is reasonable to expect that efforts to recruit blacks would succeed, an atmosphere that would encompass many of their traditions and interests must exist. But, before that kind of atmosphere can develop, there must be a critical mass of blacks on campus. Initial attempts to resolve this dilemma were directed toward intensifying efforts to hire black faculty and to convince black high school students to enroll at our university so that the "critical mass" might be formed.

Black WIU students were sent out to predominately black high schools in the state to recruit more black students and, at first, it worked. Likewise, there was an increase in the number of black faculty who signed on partly because they were assured that increasing numbers of black students would show up in their classes. However, over time, too many black faculty left after having been at WIU for only a few years. As this frustrating regression occurred I heard some administers say words to the effect of "We tried, but there is nothing for black faculty here in Macomb." That "nothing" included "there are no young black people here for them to marry," "there are no clubs here that play their music," and "there are no restaurants here that serve their food."

There was a kernel of truth to these often-expressed beliefs. None of them were wholly without foundation. To these beliefs, one could add the actual complaints of black faculty and administrators: no barbershops and beauty parlors for black people and no stores offering hair care and cosmetic products for them (the former is still true, but not the latter). But these deficiencies became more a set of rationalizations for failures to hire and retain black faculty and administrators than sufficient reasons why black professionals declined to accept jobs at WIU or, once hired, failed to stay long.

To combat these rationalizations, some of us argued that if you want to retain black faculty and administrators they must be well paid so that, assuming the validity of arguments concerning why they left, they can travel to places like Chicago where they can encounter the cultural traditions that Macomb lacks. Paying black faculty more seemed to fit "supply and demand" logic. It had been argued that "qualified" black academics are rare (note the implicit assumption that black Ph.D.s tend to be unqualified). It followed that we should acknowledge the great demand created by the small supply through offering black professorial and administrative candidates more money. The "supply and demand" precedent had already been set: years ago the Business College had successfully convinced the administration to pay a couple of married applicants the exorbitant salary of $60,000 apiece because their expertise was rare and needed for accreditation (new faculty were being hired at 20 to 30 thousand less at the time). One of our presidents during this period accepted the supply and demand logic and promised to pay more to black candidates that all-white departments wished to hire. But, to my knowledge, it never happened. Had it happened I think I would have known about it, because a few faculty members would have loudly protested "using race as a criterion for hiring." But maybe it happened and was covered up ... little chance of that. A university is like a sieve: if anything occurs that is at all controversial it leaks out immediately.

So black faculty came and went such that by the late 1990s and early 2000s the number of black faculty receded to about what it was in the 1970s. For example, in the early to mid-2000s, the entire College of Education had only one black faculty member. Needless to say, there was much discouragement among those who sought greater diversity on campus.

But we got over it and turned to a novel strategy: introduce new courses into the curriculum that focus on diversity issues. The logic behind this tactic was that teaching about the different American ethnicities would be a step in the direction of creating a warm atmosphere for students and faculty of color. If existing black faculty could teach some sections of these courses, eventually their presence in classrooms would increase the odds that black students would be in their classes. Further, black students would have an increased likelihood of getting a class with a black professor. Finally, the new courses would provide opportunities for white students to become sensitized to issues crucial to the wellbeing of black students and black and white students would have more opportunities to interact in class. In this way, we hoped that a warmer atmosphere for black students would begin to develop. As I will cover later, these diversity classes evolved to include not just black issues, or even just matters relevant to all people of color, but also considerations relevant to many other sources of American diversity: gender, sexual orientation, age, Latin American origin, wealth status, Indian and other native American heritage, religious belief such as Jewish, Christian, Hindu, Buddhism, and Islam and more.

This new focus was more a pipe dream than an active pursuit until 1989 when J. Q. Adams joined our faculty. J.Q. is a quick-witted, high-energy guy who is among the most articulate and compelling speakers I've ever encountered. He immediately became a leader in the university community and a model for black students. J. Q. and Jan Welsch became the progenitors of our diversity curriculum.

J. Q.'s high credibility was also based on his great skills in the classroom. He manages to make students so comfortable that they were willing to say whatever comes to their minds and, at the same time, is able to steer them to controversial and touchy subjects. During the early 1990s, he obtained a grant through Governor's State University (IL) to bring television cameras into his diversity classes. In the resultant video tapes—picked up and broadcasted by PBS—he adroitly handled guests ranging from an American Indian, who initially sat stone-still and uttered nary a sound, to a neo-Nazi who asserted that "blacks are retarded" (and me when I ran out of words and had to be coaxed into saying more). Through a similar arrangement with Governor's State, one of his diversity classes was again video-taped during the early 2000s. Interviews included in the resultant tapes explored the views of several famous and infamous persons, including internationally known racist David Duke. Jan Welsch and J.Q. have co-edited and contributed to several books of readings on cultural diversity, and have recently completed a book about films depicting American cultural groups in ways ranging from mean-spirited to highly sympathetic. They also organize an annual diversity conference at WIU that has drawn speakers and participants from many US states.

When it became time to sell the new set of courses to the administration, J. Q. was too convincing to ignore. His tactfulness, firm grasp of the relevant facts, and easy use of humor commanded their attention. Soon the President and Provost were on our side, but convincing the Faculty Senate proved more difficult.

Perhaps it has been in the best interest of balance that the Faculty Senate has always included some "liberals" and some "conservatives." But that fact has made it difficult to move them toward any controversial change. In addition, at one point, it was necessary to convince both the Senate and the General Education Committee (GEC) that was charged with making needed changes in the general education curriculum. Though we had allies in both the Senate and the GEC, each stage of gaining approval for a Diversity curriculum seemed to take months of going to meetings and pleading our case. Finally, we gained a majority in the Senate, possibly partly because they grew tired of seeing us at meetings and having to listen to us. Also, when the GEC became a hurdle, Charles Helm who was chiefly responsible for getting his colleagues and the administration to make some sorely needed changes in the general education curriculum, showed strong support for the diversity portion of the curriculum changes. Beginning with the final approval of all the curriculum changes, WIU students were required to take a three-hour course in cultural diversity, either a general course initially labeled "University 210," or one of many diversity related courses already in the curriculum. Participating departments ranged from African American Studies to Geography. We won the day, but as we were to discover, the fight was not over.

It was not the first time I witnessed the power of persistence. Years earlier I accompanied some women faculty and students to Springfield to lobby for a women's rights issue. An elderly male legislator was bulking when one of the women present figured out that he thought stonewalling would be sufficient to get rid of us for good. She said to him, "If you ignore the need for this legislation, we will be back again and again." His reaction was a lesson about the impact of even threatening to be persistent: He threw his head back, sighed heavily, and began to listen.

While many people know that persistence is critical in bringing about needed change, most seem not to know that returning to the battle for the maintenance of hard-won changes is perhaps the most important part of the persistence strategy. Several times since the initial successes in the early to mid-1990s, supporters of the diversity curriculum had to return to meetings of the Senate and other bodies to plead our case again. This pattern of fighting the same battle again and again was not surprising to Essie Rutledge, who taught me by her words and her example, that even if you finally win rights that should have always been yours, get ready to return to battle repeatedly.

While many people of color know this truism, it seems that most whites do not. Perhaps, because white folks have always been in the majority in America, they think that their rights will always be protected. Think again. As of this writing, the right to privacy and the right to habeas corpus—accused people must be brought before a judge in a timely fashion so that it can be determined whether or not they are being held legally—are under attack and the mostly white Senate and House of Representatives, as well as their constituents, seem not to care. We must all learn that when some people's rights are in danger, all people's rights are imperiled.

9

Relations with Black and White Students

I taught university students for about three years during graduate school and for 37.5 years at WIU. As 40 years is a long time, no one is likely to find it surprising that I have experienced relations with students varying from "openly hostile" to "very warm and close." Of course, I have rarely experienced either extreme: in almost all cases students and I have gotten along very well. Teaching college students keeps professors intellectually and emotionally youthful and better able to participate in and contribute to the changing times. However, examination of the extremes may provide insights into some differences in the circumstances experienced by black and white students at a mostly white university, It may also partially explain why college teaching is a recommended career.

I can still picture Eboni Zamani (now) Gallaher seated in the back of the room on the first day of an early 1990s "Personality and Adjustment" class. She was at that time, and still is, a petite and personable young woman whose energetic eyes communicate both warmth and intelligence. Somehow I knew that she was not a typical student. I was to discover that she is an extraordinary person.

It was a time in my career when I was trying to "get students more involved in class." In the interest of developing group activities, I divided the class into groups that remained intact for the entire semester. Members of a group were tested together and participated in a dramatic presentation together.

Students took tests individually and then retired to some side rooms where they took the test again, this time deciding, by majority rule, which answer to each question they wanted to count toward a group score. A given student's final score on the test was a combination of their individual score and their group's score. I hoped that this method would allow students to come away from the test with the answers to most questions. And, yes, though tests were more challenging than was the case prior to this change, adding group scores to individual scores improved grades.

During group testing, I roamed from side room to side room using the Socratic method to pull answers out of students: by posing questions about an item with which students were struggling, I used what they did know about the issue it raised to lead them to the correct answer. It was in this context that I first witnessed the finesse with which Eboni facilitated group interaction. She was a natural leader. It was not just my perception: a vote by her group at the end of the semester also identified her as its leader. She has a remarkable ability to appreciate not only others' feelings during discussion, but also their perspectives on the matter under discussion. These attributes are part and parcel of high "emotional intelligence" which current research is suggesting may be as important as the kind of intelligence that is measured by the IQ test.

The dramatic presentations involved one of the many issues studied in class. By half-way through the semester the groups had chosen the issues they would explore, which included Stanley Milgram's famous "obedience to authority" experiment and methods to extinguish fear of snakes (yes, the students built a mock shock-machine and brought a snake to class). I can't remember the topic Eboni's group covered in their dramatic presentation, but I do remember the anticipation of her performance.

Some of these presentations were outstanding and some not so good. Attendance ranged from a full house to about half the class. Although the schedule was made available to students, they still tended to approach me with, "When is 'such an such' being presented?" They wanted to be there for the "good stuff," but avoid the less interesting topics. However, the query about the presentation by Eboni's group was simply, "When is Eboni going to perform?" Her comments in class convinced students that her group's presentation would feature her and be special. Both assumptions were correct.

I became Eboni's mentor. Though I've played that role vis-à-vis other students, with no other has it been so rewarding and enlightening. Paula and I have watched as Eboni grew into a remarkable woman who is already having major impact as a professional. However, not all has been sweetness and light. There were times when I felt that Eboni's outstanding social skills were both a blessing and a curse. I worried that the great amount of time she spent with friends was limiting study time.

Nevertheless, Eboni finished her undergraduate and masters degrees at Western in fine style. She earned her Ph.D. degree at the University of Illinois and took a first job at West Virginia University. There she established herself as an expert on liaison between community colleges and four-year colleges and universities. Within that context she has been especially interested in problems unique to students of color as they navigate the waters of higher education.

Today Eboni is a professor at Eastern Michigan University. She chose EMU partly to be nearer her family and her graduate school sweetheart Dr. James Gallagher, a Human Resources executive with General Motors. They married during 2003 and now have two sweet and beautiful daughters, Nia and Nala.

Eboni has always tended to give others too much credit for her own success. This orientation is not without credibility. Her mother, grandmother, and father certainly were the most important people in her life. The good models they represented and the unfailing support they provided were very important in shaping the person she has become. That fact was underlined by the extraordinary sense of loss she suffered when her mother and grandmother passed away within a year of one another. Her sense of closeness to them was unparalleled. Yet, Eboni deserves the lion's share of credit for who she became. It was her resilience in the face of tragedy, her perseverance when events conspired against her, and her optimistic orientation to everything that got her to where she is.

That's the positive end of the relations with students scale. The negative end involved some shouting matches. When students got in my face, I got back in theirs. Good form? Definitely not! All you would-be professors out there, don't do as I did; it won't get you tenure.

However, that was the way it was and examining it may provide some insights. I'll illustrate with a case involving a white student and one with a black student, both female (more males than females were involved in these altercations—in my early through mid-career, most students were male, later, females became more numerous—and certainly there were many more white than black students—the portion of black students never exceeded 10%).

Some 15 years ago one of my classes contained a strikingly attractive, young, black woman who informed me that she wanted to be a flight attendant. My relations with her were routine for most of the semester, but near the end we had a disagreement about the content of her term paper. One day after class when there were just a couple of other students remaining, she began to shout at me about my refusal to accept the proposed content of her paper. One of the remaining students was an Army Special Forces officer whose duties included training soldiers to jump out of airplanes. I shouted back, initiating a thunderous argument that must have lasted several minutes. The Special Forces officer had done some research with a colleague and me, so, I knew him quite well. He was not the kind of person to be shocked by much of anything. However, the angry exchange between the student and I readily passed his shock threshold. He looked stunned.

After a time, she calmed down and so did I. I stuck by my assessment regarding what should be in her paper, and she vowed not to comply with my judgment. Showdown came when I returned her graded paper. It was actually quite good and included most of the material I thought was appropriate for her topic, given the context of the course. As I recall, she received a "B." When she found out about the grade her response was mild. I never heard from her again.

The second case occurred in a cultural diversity class (these classes sometimes were in danger of turning into riots, as I will support later). Again the bone of contention was a term paper. All students had to write about their experiences with diversity. Inevitably, many of the white students would think of diversity as involving only one dimension—black-white—and complain, "I came from a small rural town [or an all-white suburb of Chicago] and don't know any black people." I tried to point out that there were many other dimensions of human cultural diversity. Although historically, the black-white dimension has probably had the most impact on American culture, now we should also be considering "brown-yellow." Why? Earlier than predicted, Latinos have become the largest minority and the Asian population is growing at a fast rate. Then there are the alternatives I listed earlier: for example, male-female, young-old, poor-rich and so forth. After going through these alternatives, a young white woman student and I decided that she could report on her relations with black students on campus.

Her paper was truly astounding. She reported several incidents during which she claimed to have been mistreated by black students. In one case, she described how some black males had jumped on the hood of her car at a stop sign and threatened her and other students in the car. There was something suspicious about her description of this alleged event: it appeared that she may have purposely driven her car into the walk lane. Further, she went on about how the behavior she reported was "so typical of blacks" and was just the most recent of many confrontations with black people during her short life. I was thinking, "This student is a genuine bigot." But, of course, I didn't make that accusation. Instead, I wrote some questions in the margins of her paper that raised the possibility she was misinterpreting the events reported in her paper and I asked whether it made sense to generalize to all black people based on her limited experience with blacks.

Graded papers were passed out at the end of the last class session. She quickly read my comments and blew up. I was called "a f … ing SOB." Now I knew that some students didn't like me. After more than 30 years, I had taught many thousands of students; you can't please them all. Also, not too many years before this incident I found "Dr. Allen sucks" chalked on the sidewalk just outside the entrance to my building (I furtively tried to wipe it away with the sole of my shoe, but once inside the building, jocular comments by colleagues confirmed that my efforts were too late). Nevertheless, in the previous 30 some-odd years of my career I had never before suffered the indignity of being cursed to my face. I yelled back at her using strong language but no four-letter words. She left in a huff. Upon returning to class on final exam day, she meekly settled into her seat without uttering a word. This change in demeanor was probably because she described the shouting match to one of my colleagues, who reported to me that he told her something to the effect of "that was a dumb thing to do." The whole incident was a tempest in a teapot: the "C" I assigned her paper could have been an "F" and it would not have changed her grade.

These are just two cases out of the admittedly very small number of shouting matches I've had with black and white students. So, the sample is small and unrepresentative, but I can't help seeing a difference between the reactions of black and white students to being involved in a shouting match. In altercations with black students the shouting was typically followed by a calming-down period and a resolution of the problem. White students seemed to get angrier, more stubborn, and less amenable to compromise as the altercation continued. Maybe I've stumbled upon a cultural difference … maybe not.

There was once a student who yelled loudly at me about his test grades as we emerged from class into a crowded hallway. In my memory, that was the only time I ever allowed a student to dress me down and not respond. His case brings up an important issue relating to diversity.

I knew that he was dying of cystic fibrosis. He had told me that both he and his twin sister had the disease and that she was already deceased. He was struggling with grief over the loss of his sister, his own inevitable fate, and his frustration at not being able to lead a normal life. I could think of nothing to say.

This young man taught me an important lesson. I've found that people can get into arguments about who is most oppressed, my group or your group. During the 1980s, when almost the entire university administration and most of the faculty were white males—not to mention officials of national, state, and local government—white male students in one of our colleges nominated themselves as the most oppressed group on campus. Although we can all make a case that people like ourselves have suffered undeserved misfortune, if we are at all fair-minded, we should be able to acknowledge that the plight of some other groups may be worse than that of our own group. In any case, if we possess more than a modicum of empathy, we will all understand that there are no winners in the "most oppressed" contest. There are many people whose extraordinary misfortune cannot be seen in their skin color, hair texture or other facial features; you have to listen to them talk about their lives. When you do you will find individuals like the young man who was destined to die of cystic fibrosis.

I had other students like him. One tearfully informed me that she had just been diagnosed with cancer. She was about 20 years old. I never would have suspected that she was facing such an oppressive future. Another was undergoing chemotherapy and had lost her hair. She told me that she would have to leave class periodically because she would become ill. Though she was usually present in class and completed the course, other students seemed not to notice her dreadful condition. The more people know about other's lives the more sure they will be that they are not unique in being unfairly victimized by conditions beyond their control.

Oppression takes other forms. In the early 1970s I was talking to a young woman student. She told me of her travels, many by hitchhiking, a common practice among young adults at that time. Suddenly she disclosed that a man had raped her after she had accepted a ride from him. She didn't cry and her voice didn't falter, but her tone was at the same time both mournful and matter-of-fact. I imagined that she had come to believe there is no way to prevent awful things from happening to good people for no good reason.

10

Adventures in Diversity Class

By the beginning of the mid-1990s our diversity (multicultural) curriculum was implemented and I taught the general course, University 210 (later it became Arts and Sciences 210). I really didn't know how to proceed. Straight lecture was out. Because the body of knowledge under consideration is heterogeneous, sometimes controversial, and likely to stimulate expressions of personal opinions and experiences, class discussion had to be the focus. I thought we'd spend part of the time discussing assignments in a book of readings (later handouts were added). The rest of the time we would watch videos with stops for discussion about every 10 to 15 minutes.

On the first day of the first class, Tiffany, as I will call her, made a grand entrance. As she sauntered from the door to the front of the room, she rolled up her sleeve and exclaimed, "See this dark skin ... I'm black!" Tiffany was to become the center of almost everything that happened of any importance during that semester.

So we watched videos and the students reacted variously. Some went to sleep. Others read something from their backpacks and still others passed notes to students in neighboring seats. I responded by shortening the video-watching-interval to 5–10 minutes, but the substantial minority of disinterested students threatened to become a majority. After only a few classes, Tiffany loudly announced, "I refuse to see any more videos; we want to talk!" Several students nodded in agreement. The rebellion was under way.

I said, "Ok, let's talk." I don't remember exactly what was said thereafter, but it involved charges and counter-charges. Tiffany implied that "whites are racists" and some white students took offense. She was condemned with words like the following: "You don't even know me; how can you call me prejudiced; you're the one who's prejudiced!" The few other black students lamely came to Tiffany's defense, but basically she was subjected to an overwhelming barrage of complaints.

Finally, a white male student told Tiffany to "shut up!" At that point I intervened. I had announced on the first day that students should all feel free to express their opinions no matter how inflammatory or controversial they might be. The first amendment was to be fully actualized in our class. The offending student was told to apologize, which he did, begrudgingly.

Following that explosive day, the class settled down ... somewhat. Controversial issues examined in class raised the hair on the backs of many necks: American Indians, shown in a video, taking over and trashing the Bureau of Indian Affairs in Washington, D. C. and a gay writer of an assigned article claiming the right to marry. There were heated debates back and forth, but everyone got to speak her or his mind.

As the semester wore on, Tiffany lightened up. She became the first of many students in the class over the years to announce that one of her parents was black and the other white. A great deal of her upset was generated by an "identity crisis." Some black students, who either had a white parent or had been reared by whites, were understandably conflicted over their racial identity. Tiffany, as it turned out, had transferred from a university in her home state, Mississippi. Because she "looked black," everyone she encountered treated her as "black." Not surprisingly she talked the talk and walked the walk. Her major problem was what probably afflicts many, but not all, "mixed" blacks: she didn't want to totally deny her "white ancestry," lest she denounce her white parent.

By the end of the semester, I, and many of the students, came to respect and like Tiffany. She proved to be bright, insightful, and a poet of considerable talent. I think she was attempting to reciprocate my positive feelings about her when she shared some of her poems with me. I was honestly able to tell her that her writings were very good.

My perceptions of the young man who told her to "shut up" also changed. His confrontation with Tiffany and some of his other comments made me think of him as closed-minded. However, we were in the middle of considering gay, lesbian, bi-sexual, and transgendered people when he revealed that his summer job had been in a department store with many gay personnel (transgendered people feel that they are trapped in the "wrong body"; they don't accept their assigned sex; see the movie "Transamerica"). In fact, the store was located in his hometown, which had a significant "gay" (in the generic sense) population. To my surprise, he expressed respect for many of the gay men with whom he worked and, in some cases, even admiration. Earlier he had seemed militantly "straight"; after learning more about him, he appeared to be an atypically tolerant heterosexual. It was a reminder: one should know another person at least reasonably well before making assumptions about her or him. People have even been known to make false assumptions about their spouses (attribute a stereotype to him or her for which there is not even a kernel of truth). Imagine how often they make that mistake about people they "know" only at work?

The diversity class attracted "mixed" race blacks like a magnet. Many enrolled in part to find out "who am I?" Not even in South Africa are people with "one drop of black blood" classified as "black." They are called "coloured" and traditionally were afforded more rights than people who are known to have only African heritage. In the USA, though, if a person who has one discernable characteristic that is "African" (for example, hair like lamb's wool, or broad nose, or dark skin) she or he is classed as "black" by almost all whites (and many blacks), unless some cultural cue—such as language, accent, or dress—places their family origin outside Sub-Saharan Africa. Included in this group are almost all "blacks" adopted by white parents (most such adoptees have known European heritage; the rest are likely to have ancestors from Europe, because it is estimated that as many as 70% of all African Americans have European heritage).

Sometimes "mixed students" in the diversity course were merely curious about how black and white students would react to the revelation that one or both of their parents were white. Most seemed to be clearly self-identified as "black." However, there were some "mixed" diversity students, and several I have encountered outside of the university context, who were clearly not firmly identified as "black." A Hispanic diversity-course student with African features was not only not self-identified as "black," but was also genuinely confused that others thought of him as "black." Near the end of one class session, in front of the other students, he actually asked me to tell him what it is to be "black." I was so confounded that I literally exclaimed, "Class dismissed." During the next class session we dealt with the fact that being "black" (or Jewish or Iranian, etc.) is much too complex to be expressed even in enough words to fill up a long book (Ralph Ellison's "Invisible Man" (1952) is an entire book about "being black" but some blacks, then and now, say that he got it wrong). After the discussion, many of the other students seemed to understand the complexity of "being black" (or embracing any other ethnic identity), but the young Hispanic student appeared to be even more disconcerted than before.

"Hispanic White" and "Hispanic Non-white" are in common use today and refer to people of Spanish ancestry who were either born in Spain or whose families originated from Spain (Cubans and people whose ancestors date to the Conquistadores) and people with Native American and/or black ancestry as well as Spanish ancestry, respectively. A good example of the latter is Dr. Samuel Betances, a Puerto Rican scholar and lecturer whose humorous and insightful talks and articles shed much light on "the Latino experience" and on issues of race. Having watched videos featuring him and read articles by him it seems to me that his primary source of identity is Puerto Rican, but he is also very proud of both his African and Spanish ancestry. He makes it clear that "Hispanic" is a rubric defining a group of such enormous diversity that it can't be characterized as a whole on any dimension one can name. The only strong impression I have of the many millions of people falling under the heading "Hispanic" is that their "nation of origin," or that of their parents and grandparents, is almost always an important part of their identities.

I can recall only one "mixed" black student with one or two white parents who appeared fully identified as "black" (there were others who provided so little information about themselves in class and in their term papers to allow for any conclusion about their degree of identity as "black"). This student had two white parents, neither his biological parent. The way he spoke, what he said, how he dressed, and most importantly, the fact that he hung out with and was clearly accepted by other black students made me believe that he was fully identified as "black."

But isn't being "half" white or having white parents (or both) a source of confusion on the part of "mixed" blacks? One would think so. After all, even though the "one drop rule" was imposed on African Americans, to function reasonably smoothly in the USA they have to acknowledge the reality of it. The problem is that mixed black people not reared by black parents may not know "how to be black." I know of several cases for which black children and teens not reared by black parents attempted to learn how to be black (again, the sample is small and unrepresentative). In the case of one "black" female college student with two white parents, attempts to be accepted by black students at her school failed. In another case, a black college student with two white parents corrected the English of black students on his campus. Needless to say, that did not work; he gave up all efforts "to be black."

Do "mixed blacks" who are afforded no opportunity for immersion into black culture during childhood and adolescence end up with ambiguous senses of identity and accompanying psychological problems? Anecdotal accounts, and one TV documentary on the subject, seem to suggest an affirmative answer. However, the only solid psychological study on this issue that I've seen indicated that black children adopted into white households turned out very well up to the age of 13 (where the study ended), though they may have gone through periods of identity confusion (most such adoptions involve "mixed" black children). When you think about it, that they were doing well in life makes sense. To meet adoption criteria, candidate parents have to have middle class or upper middle class status. Adoptive parents who are financially secure or affluent can provide for their adoptees' material requirements as well as their educational needs, including the provision of a higher education. Based on the little information available about the subject, anguish over personal identity, even if it occurs for many if not most "mixed" blacks, does not preclude ending up with a "good life" as we define it in the USA. If you want more information about "Who is Black?" see F. James Davis' book with that title (subtitled "One Nation's Definition"). It is a very surprising and totally fascinating book. An Oprah show entitled "What is your Race?" includes an interview with Dr. Davis and is the best capsule consideration of race I can name (one of the revelations Oprah made during this show was that some 28,000,000 "white" Americans have African heritage and don't know it; Davis cut that figure in half during a telephone conversation with me).

Another category of students enrolled in the diversity course encompasses people who have multiple ethnic identities and are "black" only from other people's perspectives. For example, a student from the Caribbean who spoke with a British accent, declared herself to be Irish, Jewish and, yes, black. In cherishing all of her identities, and refusing to choose which was most important to her, she represents a growing population in the USA. Millions of Americans, many with African heritage, checked several categories on the recent U. S. Census survey, or declined to check any. This category of people is likely to grow.

On a few occasions white students behaved in an openly racist manner during diversity class sessions. One such case involved a very small class, five white students and two black students. Two white males tended to sneer at whatever the black students contributed to class discussion, but they never overtly responded to anything the black students said. Because I was facing them, I could see their more subtle reactions but the other students could not. One day when both black students were absent, I was trying to make a point about the stereotype that "black people are criminals." Without correction for poverty and racism, it is true that the proportion of black people who are convicted of crimes is greater than that for whites (hidden "white collar" crime and bias in the courts are also not controlled). But, in fact, and contrary to statements by some public figures, only a small percentage of blacks commit crimes. To make that point I asked, "What percentage of blacks commit crimes?" Some of the white students' responses were reasonable: 5%, 10%. However, the two guys who had remained silent in the presence of the black students chimed in with 90%, 95%. I was so caught by surprise and so angry that what I said was too ineffectual to wipe the grins off these two guys' faces. When the black students returned, these two cowards regressed to sneering silence.

Something similar happened to a black colleague in his diversity class when he had to miss a session and a white colleague filled in. The surprised substitute reported that several blatantly racist comments were made during the class session. There had been no such expressions earlier.

Another diversity class included a white male student from Chicago who was a proud member of a white ethnic group. He indicated that his neighborhood bordered on a black community and that he and his friends had been involved in numerous conflicts with their black neighbors. Unlike the two deceptive white males, this guy openly expressed his feelings about blacks. For example, he once volunteered that "they [blacks] throw their babies out of their high-rise building windows." While some students were angry with him and others rolled their eyes when he talked, even the black students seemed to respect his willingness to state his feelings openly rather than attempt to hide his biases. So we all allowed him to speak his mind and we used what he said to learn more about prejudice. This guy talked of literally physically fighting with blacks all of his life, just as his friends had and just as his father had. It soon became apparent that, if people are immersed in racism from an early age, it will be very difficult for them to grow up fair-minded.

There were also some disturbing reactions to the gay people who visited class (again, "gay" is used generically for gay, lesbian, bisexual, and trans-gendered). In the early 1990s gay students were virtually invisible. So, if I wanted to provide students with some insight into what it is like to be gay in our society, the only resources I had were the few gay faculty and staff I happened to know. On one occasion, I invited a couple of gay male colleagues to visit class and talk about their experiences. The students reacted politely but sat in stony silence. About mid-way through the session one of the male students addressed the visitors with words to the effects of, "Tell us why you do sex the way you do it." I was stunned; the guests were embarrassed. After a few moments of uncomfortable silence, I remarked, "It's none of your business." I'm sure I could have chosen other comments that would have been more productive, but once the bomb blew up, I doubt that there were any words that would have saved the day.

Another class included a small, thin male student who said nothing much and showed little reaction to anything all semester. But when gay visitors showed up to class, he became very agitated and looked like he would, at any moment, jump up and flee. He managed to restrain himself until the end of the class, when he did, in fact, sprint to the door. It was the best lesson on homophobia—literally, fear of gays—I can recall, but it was lost on the students, many of whom were too busy dealing with their confused feelings to notice that one of their own was about to explode.

From the late-1990s to mid-2000s, the gay student organization on campus, now called Unity, became prominent and actively sought to visit classes. This organization was a main reason why tolerance for and understanding of gay people increased compared to earlier years. Unity students often began a visitation by having class members come up with all the derogatory references to gays they could conjure. All of these derisive words and phrases were written up on the board. Just displaying these "forbidden" words made the visitors seem cool and able to laugh at themselves. In addition, it so de-sensitized the students that they relaxed and expressed their own feelings about gay people.

A number of informative observations resulted from these student visits. For example, "the Bible condemns being gay" became the one position that seemed unassailable. All people are entitled to their religious beliefs. In terms of religious beliefs, it's true for you because you believe it. The Bible does condemn being gay in a few places, but it also would punish adultery with death by stoning, and harshly condemns wearing jewelry or cloth composed of more than one kind of fabric. If we obeyed the stoning command we'd run out of rocks. But what about complying with the commands regarding jewelry and cloth (and other universally violated commands)? Why are we so selective in honoring some of these Biblical edicts and not others?

Another observation I've made based on experiences in class is that women are much more tolerant of gays than are men. This one happens to be backed by some current research. Why is that? Women are generally more tolerant? Or is it that femininity is more flexible than masculinity? Though exclusively lesbian women are a smaller proportion of the female population than the percentage of men who are exclusively gay, women are known to touch, hug, and kiss each other—as well as dabble in same-gender sex—much more than men. Perhaps intimate physical contact with the same gender is more threatening to a man's masculinity than it is to a women's femininity.

There were some broad, general issues that periodically cropped up in class. One of the most far-reaching in its implications can be stated as a question: Are all cultures "good?" For me the answer is, yes, all cultures are "good." Therefore, we should honor and respect all of them. However, all cultures are a set of very complex of practices, traditions, and beliefs. Any entity of that nature will have its "bad" aspects. The general USA culture is rightly known for the traditions of generosity, self-sufficiency, and ingenuity as well as numerous other positive attributes. Nevertheless, our culture has its down side. Because of our history, racism is a part of our culture.

Other cultures are also rightly lauded for their many positive attributes. But they also will have negative attributes. Thus, it is worse than nonsense for anyone to claim that one should never say anything bad about any culture. Some people not only make that ridiculous claim, but they have gone on to say that cultures are not good or bad, just different; we should accept all aspects of each culture, without question.

If one assumes that there are some universal human rights, as does Amnesty International, violation of those rights is absolutely unacceptable regardless of what cultural imperative is invoked to justify the abuse. "Bad," then, includes, but is not limited to, violation of the rights of all human beings to have shelter and sufficient nourishment to sustain life, to be protected from imprisonment without due process, to never experience having anything done to their bodies without their consent, and to express their points of view freely, without repercussions.

Perhaps the most widespread "bad" side of too many cultures is the subjugation of women and girls. When female babies are considered undesirable, girls are denied an education, women are burned to death because their husbands' families view their dowries as insufficient, women who have been raped are killed by family members for "dishonoring the family" or are forced to marry the rapist (who receives a minimum penalty, if any), husbands are allowed or even encouraged to beat their wives and are treated leniently should they kill their wives, cultural imperatives are no defense. Neither is there a cultural defense for declaring some people to be "sub-human" or "untouchable."

Is there any group of people numbering in the millions that is constituted by mostly "good" or mostly "bad" people? Obviously the question is absurd. However, sometimes the "obvious" may escape us. There was a period during the 1960s when Hollywood depicted black people as "all good" (see the movie "Guess Who's Coming to Dinner"). Interestingly, this period was short-lived and followed by "black exploitation" movies promoting the impression that the most pervasive trait of black men is "violent" (in some ways this depiction continues today). In fact, current psychological research shows that the stereotype of black men as violent helps to explain why New York City police shot at an unarmed black man 41 times, hitting him 19 times and killing him. Further, this stereotype may be so non-consciously and strongly harbored by most whites and some blacks that its effects can be recorded in the brain. My own research shows that the stereotype may cause memory distortions that may have dire implications for black men.

So it appears that we can "know the obvious" and yet have it slip our minds under some circumstances. "Obviously," every large group of people includes both saints and psychopaths, with almost all members fitting between the extremes. When we engage in "double-think"—knowing something but failing to bring it to mind when it is relevant—we may engage in or support behaviors that are clearly unacceptable. In the USA, these transgressions have ranged from the 1890 slaughter of American Indians at Wounded Knee that moved Indians closer to extinction (only about 250,000 remained alive after that attack), through supporting the internment of all main-land Japanese Americans during World War II, to condemning all Arabs after 9/11/2001, resulting in the death of one man wearing a turban who originated from India because he "looked" Arab (by the way, Arabs are a minority among Muslims). In all cases, we are reacting as if all members of these groups are "bad."

On the other side of the coin, thinking of all or most members of a large group as "good" can be worse than burdensome. Asian Americans are seen as the "model minority": they actually do better than other groups, including whites, in terms of educational attainment and household (but not per capita) income, and they are held up as models for other minorities to emulate, because they are viewed as "not causing any trouble" and hard working (lumping Japanese, Chinese, Korean, Vietnamese and other Asian groups together is widely done but it hides major differences). First, this view of Asians includes the expectations that all (or most) will succeed educationally and financially. But what if they don't meet expectations? This predicament can be appreciated by considering a specific expectation, labeled the "high tech coolie" stereotype: Asians are expected to be good at math, science, and technology. But what if an Asian man lacks skills that fit into these three categories? He would share experiences with a black man who is no good at basketball. Second, Asian Americans are successful despite biases against them, not because they have somehow received favored treatment. For example, Asians are less likely to own a house than whites, partly because they share with blacks the relative lack of a valuable legacy passed on from previous generations, an issue to which I will return. Third, holding up Asians as the "model minority" gives them a heavy burden to carry, blinds other groups to the prejudice against them, and generates conflict with groups that are taunted with "why don't you be more like Asians" (witness the strife between blacks and Koreans in Chicago). Regarding all or most members of a group as "good" is not so good. Perhaps we should avoid demonizing or canonizing all members of any large group.

There have been some issues arising in diversity class that have really gotten the students' juices flowing. One such is Peggy McIntosh's "white privilege": having "a leg up" on the road to success simply because one is white (she is white). McIntosh, whose writings became widely known during the 1990s, saw what should have been obvious to us all. Her innovative contribution occurred in part because she is a person of great insight and sensitivity. However, it took so long for "white privilege" to be acknowledged by whites, in part because white folks' unearned privilege might be in jeopardy if it were made public. Further, it is possible that white people harbor an apperception of their privileged status, but suppress it because it is an affront to their individualistic orientation: "I've worked hard and earned everything I've got. Nobody gave me anything." To sum it up, you will not see what you don't want to see: in this case, if you value having "done it all myself," you will loathe to acknowledge that your racial identity is a factor in your success. In any case, "white privilege" is manifested with enough subtlety that white people might miss it. When McIntosh's point of view was considered in class, some white students reacted as if they were as blind, deaf, and dumb as the infamous three "see no evil, hear no evil, speak no evil" monkeys. Finally, it is certain that some blacks did try to tell whites about "white privilege," though they used different terms, but it is easy to believe that their words fell on deaf ears.

Convincing white students that they are privileged has been a daunting task. They honestly don't see that they have a leg up. For example, one has to acknowledge that, all things being equal, whites are more likely to be hired before getting to the question, "Why are whites more likely to be hired?" A strong candidate for a good answer was aptly illustrated on an episode of television's 20/20: blacks are less likely to be hired because whites are doing the hiring. Bosses, historically and continually, are white males who have looked at an applicant and, mostly non-consciously, see the would-be employee as acceptable to the degree that the candidate is "like us." Little wonder that they so often choose white male candidates.

Another reason that unearned privilege remains unacknowledged is that whites fail to appreciate the fact that their families have had many generations to accumulate wealth, whereas black families have had at most a few generations. Blacks have found most doors to wealth locked shut until the 1960's. This type of blindness to advantage suggests a principle that is broad enough to apply to rich versus poor regardless of race: Gloria Steinem once said, "Rich people plan for four generations. Poor people plan for Saturday night." It makes little sense to plan for future generations if one currently has few resources.

"Wealth" per se is not the only issue. Having the means to attend superior K-12 and secondary schools generates the expectation that one's children will also go far in school. Expectations are powerful. Historically, most black parents did not expect of their children what had been nearly impossible for the progeny of black parents during earlier generations.

Peggy McIntosh didn't stop with "white privilege." She has also pointed out male privilege (benefits enjoyed by males but denied females) and "heterosexual privilege" (benefits enjoyed by heterosexual people but denied gay people).

"Reparations" is another contentious issue that I've brought up not only in diversity class but also in other classes, beginning with those I taught in my first years at WIU. "Reparations" may be translated as "repair to people what they have lost through no fault of their own." Reparations have been meted-out many times in the history of the USA. The most pervasive example has been well-deserved reparations provided to armed forces veterans. The rationale has been that veterans, often at great peril to themselves, have given up jobs and been separated from their families to serve in our name. Thus, when the service is over, veterans are given priority in hiring, money for college educations, and low cost home loans. Another example is the relatively recent payment of $20,000 per Japanese American family whose relatives were interned in camps during WWII while, in many cases, their businesses and other property was permanently deeded to other citizens.

While most people are pleased to grant these benefits to veterans—as well they should be—some white students go ballistic at the mere suggestion that black people might be entitled to reparations, because they have been denied opportunities available to other citizens throughout most of the history of the USA. One frequently advanced argument against reparations for blacks goes something like this: "Just because some people have had a hard time doesn't mean they should be compensated for it. My ancestors came here from Ireland [or Italy or Germany or ...] without a penny in their pockets. They managed to make it by working hard. They didn't get any reparations." Another argument was that "Discrimination happened a long time ago. Why should I pay more taxes for reparations to people who now have the same opportunities as everyone else?" Of course, these arguments ignore everything discussed about "white privilege" and the observation, considered above, that past discrimination of a people can generate a ripple effect of tidal wave proportions during the lives of their descendents (for example, deficits in wealth accumulation and home ownership).

Only recently has reparations for blacks been seriously considered in the media. It came to light that some still existing businesses benefited from slavery. For example, some insurance companies laid the foundation for their continued existence and success by insuring slaves. It was argued that those companies owed reparations to the ancestors of slaves. Lawsuits were proposed that, given success in the courts, would have resulted in educational funds for blacks paid for by businesses that insured slaves. Young black people could claim support from these funds to finance their college educations. As of this writing, nothing has come from legal attempts to generate reparations.

I once made a rough calculation of how much it would cost to fund reparations to black families. Let's just put it this way: the cost of reparations to black families paid at the rate dispensed to Japanese American families would be trivial compared to the cost of several months of the war in Iraq. Further, if the money were earmarked for education, it would generate so much success among future generations of black people, their taxes would more than pay it back. Is this an outlandish proposal? Recent efforts by Bill and Melinda Gates make it seem not so out of line. Though reparation may not have been on their minds, they have donated one billion dollars to fund minority scholarships. That billion will become multibillions over time.

11

Guilt is Good

White college students, as a group, are very open-minded and are becoming more so as time goes by. That being said, I can sum up the end of the last chapter succinctly: they tend to deny any responsibility for oppression stemming from prejudice and discrimination, and, thus, feel no guilt regarding it. It seemed ineffectual to point out that their parents, grandparents, and great grandparents probably practiced discrimination and that the "good life" they enjoy today may have, in part, been delivered to them on the backs of black people. A typical response was something like this: "That was then, this is now. Racism is over now, and I'm not responsible for whatever my relatives may have done in the past." Still, I find it hard to believe that they don't feel guilt about their ancestors' complicity in racism. We identify with our ancestors as indicated by the pride we take in their accomplishments. Sometimes we talk of their power, achievements, and good deeds as if those credits belong to us. Surely we feel some guilt about their bad deeds.

If so, what are the implications? Before answering that question, it is important to consider the nature of "guilt." Psychological researchers Jessica Tracy and Richard Robins have recently differentiated guilt from shame. In the case of guilt we feel that we have been involved in relatively controllable events that resulted in wrongdoing. As a result we experience the need to confess and apologize. In contrast, we feel shame when we have been involved in relatively uncontrollable events that resulted in wrongdoing. Accordingly we feel the need to escape the scene of the event and avoid reference to it. Behaviorally, shame promotes fleeing and hiding, negative or withdrawing kinds of behaviors, while guilt promotes approach and reparation, positive or approaching behaviors (researchers have actually used "reparation" in reference to how people may respond to guilt). Therefore, guilt is "good" because it promotes positive, pro-social behavior. Further, ever since Freud wrote about it, "conscience" has been all about feeling bad when one has done wrong. Thus, it is reasonable to argue that guilty feelings are a sign that one has a conscience and, since having a conscious is "good," so is guilt. Raise your hand if you agree. Not all hands went up.

Some people seem to think that acknowledging guilt is inviting indictment. Because admitting to guilt may be seen as confessing to wrongdoing, some people effectively claim not to feel guilty about much of anything (and not all of them are politicians). To others, feeling guilty is being weak. "Strong" people manage to reinterpret their wrongs in order to transform them into rights.

So who would you rather relate to: A. a person who denies guilt lest she or he be accused of wrongdoing, B. a person who admits to doing what most people would see as wrong, but "gets in your face" and declares that what is objectively wrong is actually right, or C. a person who admits to wrongdoing, confesses guilty feelings, and seeks to make amends?

Obviously, most of us sometimes behave in ways that put us in the A or B categories. Occasionally, or even frequently, circumstances may seem to force us into behavior that defines A and B. Perhaps we rarely fit into C, but most of us would acknowledge that we would be better human beings if we more often met C criteria.

Given this background, imagine how I felt when in the early 1990s I found out for sure what I had always suspected: at least one of my relatives had owned slaves. A cousin, Carolyn Allen Alevra, extensively researched the genealogy of the Allens (my father's side), Prices (my mother's side), and other branches of our family (remember: the Prices and the Allens were related). She discovered that Washington Price, father of the first Bem Price, was a slave owner. As I had years to think about it prior to knowing it for sure, it was relatively easy to be a C. I felt guilty, still do, and am glad of it. I think that the premonition my family included slave-owners is **one** of the reasons I've chosen the course my life has taken.

Sadly, slavery is thriving today. Recently it was estimated that slavery is more widespread in the 21st Century than ever before. But the victims have changed. Boys as young as age seven have been conscripted into militias all over the world by terrorists, revolutionaries, and drug dealers. Girls and young women are being kidnapped and forced into prostitution sometimes in their home countries (including in the USA), but often in some foreign land. So, perhaps the largest segment of today's slaves ranges in age from less than 10 to less than 20. Adult slaves are spirited out of their home countries into slavery as laborers who are barely paid or fed and are not allowed to leave their work sites.

If you have done nothing about modern slavery and feel guilty, good for you. I've done nothing substantive about it myself. Thus, let's put guilt to good use and find out what we can do to stop slavery. Start by Googling (or Ask ing) "modern slavery."

Epilogue

◆

Students are Good

Because I've written about conflicts with students, as well as good relations with them, I want to be clear that the latter characterized my experiences with them. The number of students enrolled in my classes over the 40 years I've taught is in five figures. The number with whom there has been appreciable conflict numbers in at most three figures, maybe even two. Mainly I've been blessed with open, thoughtful, humane students, who were a pleasure to be around. I'm in communication with some of them to this day. Not so long ago I recommended the professorial life to readers of a Peoria Journal Star article who were looking for a rewarding professional life for themselves or their children (November, 28, 2004, page A5). In my case, because of students—as well as colleagues/friends and administrators—life as a professor has been marvelous. In order to emphasize that I have great respect and affection for my students I have dedicated this book to them.

I would like to invite you to tell me about your experiences with race. I'll be interested in what you have to say regardless of your race or ethnicity. You can communicate whatever actual events relating to race that have occurred to you during your life and how they have impacted you emotionally and otherwise; I want you to be candid and I will not judge you. While I will ask you to give me consent to use all or part of what you have to say, so that it will be eligible for possible use in a forthcoming book, I guarantee your anonymity: I will not reveal your identity in the book or to anyone, anywhere. I will ask you for your race or ethnicity, age, and gender and that information will be used in the book.

Below, you will find a link to a web site where you can record your experiences with race and send them to me. The space will be limited; I hope you can be concise. However, if you have more to say than space allows, please TYPE it out and send it to Bem Allen, Psychology 110, Western Illinois University, Macomb, IL 61455.

http://www.wiu.edu/users/mfbpa/experienceswithrace.html

978-0-595-44492-2
0-595-44492-X

www.ingramcontent.com/pod-product-compliance
Lightning Source LLC
Chambersburg PA
CBHW051421280526
45785CB00003B/1112